Globalization and Social Change

Globalization and Social Change

Ellina Samantroy
Indu Upadhyay

Rawat Publications
Jaipur • New Delhi • Bangalore • Hyderabad • Guwahati

ISBN 978-81-316-0536-3

Published by
Prem Rawat for **Rawat Publications**
Satyam Apts, Sector 3, Jawahar Nagar, Jaipur 302 004 (India)
Phone: 0141 265 1748 / 7006 Fax: 0141 265 1748
E-mail: info@rawatbooks.com
Website: www.rawatbooks.com

New Delhi Office
4858/24, Ansari Road, Daryaganj, New Delhi 110 002
Phone: 011 2326 3290

Also at *Bangalore, Hyderabad* and *Guwahati*

Typeset by Rawat Computers, Jaipur
Printed at Chaman Enterprises, New Delhi

To the Almighty
and
our families

Contents

List of Tables

List of Figures

Acknowledgements

This volume is an outcome of various national and international conferences held across the country. Most of the papers included in this volume were earlier presented at these conferences and a great deal of collective effort has been put into this project since then. We are grateful to many individuals and institutions for inviting us to present some of these papers at conferences. They include Professor A.K. Pandey, Director, Centre for Exclusion and Inclusive Policy, Banaras Hindu University, The Indian Sociological Society, and Indian Economic Association, New Delhi.

This book reflects a collaborative work of two scholars having different ways of looking at the same reality. It is a sincere effort both on our parts to have an interdisciplinary and diverse understanding of the complex issue of globalization. Last but not the least, we would like to thank each other for cooperation and support without which this work would not have been possible.

Introduction

Like most developing countries, India followed a path of self-reliant planned development after independence. This was a conscious choice of political economy, expected from a strong nationalist political leadership which had just won independence from colonial dominance. India adopted large-scale public investment to provide a big push to industrialization. As the entire development strategy had hinged on public investment as an engine of growth, large fiscal deficits arising from excessive government spending began to shake the macro-economic balance. India seemed to be caught in a low equilibrium trap of the so-called 3.5 per cent Hindu rate of growth. Although the GDP growth did pick up to almost 6 per cent level in the 1980s, this was driven by a massive expansion in the country's fiscal deficit. The growing structural imbalance in the economy, the current account deficit climbed over 2 per cent of GDP by the end of 1980s, which led to a severe balance of payment crisis in July 1991. India adopted New

Economic Policy in 1991 under the pressure of World Bank/IMF. It aimed at harnessing the externalities of competitive efficiency for the process of economic development.

Globalization (structural reforms) aimed at allowing a greater interplay of a market-driven process of resource allocation and pricing. This involved the dismantling of industrial licensing, price controls and an infusion of completion through the introduction of a larger number of companies, including foreign companies. It also aimed at integrating the Indian economy with the global system and enhancing its robustness through wider access to better technology and benchmarking with the global performers. The complete impact of the reform measures edges into view over a long span of time. Nevertheless, a period of nearly two decades since the introduction of the reform process is long enough to make visible the results of reforms. Therefore, the book aims at studying the impact of structural reforms on the Indian society. Since structural reforms have affected many sectors of the economy and society, it is difficult to study them all. So, the book is divided into two sections, namely, Globalization and Economic Life and Globalization and Socio-cultural Change. Both the sections have four chapters each.

The first chapter *Globalization, Structural Reforms and Its Impact on Indian Agriculture* is a comparative analysis of the performance of agriculture in pre-reform and post-reform India. Not only globalization has contributed to the overall growth of the economy but also provided employment and food security to majority of the population in the country. Further, the chapter looks into the causes behind the decline in the growth rate of agriculture and finally suggests various measures to solve the problem. This chapter also provides an overview of the issues and policies, the impact of structural macro-economic policy reforms on agriculture and reforms relating to supply side factor in the agriculture sector. Structural reforms in agriculture have both positive and negative effects.

Agriculture got benefited indirectly due to overprotection given to the industry in the post-reform period. The terms of trade, private investment, opportunities for technology and specialization have increased for agriculture. On the negative side, trade reforms might have affected some crops and increased dependence on global prices which are volatile. Fiscal and financial liberalization also had some adverse impact on investments and credit. It has been concluded by some that the slowdown in agriculture is linked directly to structural reforms in the country and globalization including joining of WTO.

The second chapter *Food Security and Globalization in India* throws light on the need for food subsidy in India. It needs no emphasis that while the structural adjustment programmes have brought about some reduction in consumer food subsidies, the impact of such reductions, as a rule, has been small. Most prominent among the reasons is that unlike the food subsidies in South Asia, Latin America and Eastern Europe, subsidies in Africa did not effectively deliver cheap food to the vulnerable households. Where subsidies were prevalent, they rarely reached the poor; instead they were highly rationed to the benefits of civil servants, professional workers and the well-to-do in the urban areas. The chapter also examines whether the demand and supply of food grains are equal or not and finally, it suggests various measures for getting rid of the evils of the public distribution system (PDS).

The third chapter *Poverty and Globalization* studies the problem of poverty after the adoption of economic reforms. Further, in this regard, social welfare aimed at development or improvement in the well-being of the people which is an important objective of development planning. No doubt, economic growth is extremely important but it has to be accompanied by improvement in the quality of life of the people for the development process to be sustainable in the long run. The motion of inclusive growth relates essentially to equality of opportunity to all for productive and meaningful life with freedom and dignity. In terms of policy measures, it requires emphasis on social sector development and programmes. The development of human resources contributes to sustained growth and productive employment. A healthy, educated and skilled workforce can more significantly and effectively contribute to economic development. Therefore, the chapter is an attempt to study poverty in India and the indicators selected for the purpose are human development, equality, hunger and unemployment.

The fourth chapter *Globalization and the Banaras Silk Industry: A Case Study of Weavers of Banaras* focuses on the detrimental effects of globalization on the Indian weaving industry and the increased competition in the Indian market between the foreign and domestic companies. With the foreign commodities being cheaper than the Indian goods, the consumer preferred to buy them. This reduced the amount of profits of the Indian industrial units. This chapter makes an attempt to study the crisis faced by the weavers of Banarasi sarees. This chapter makes the result of an empirical study done from various areas of Varanasi city where weavers of Banarasi sarees live. Further, it analyses various problems faced by the weavers and the causes behind them. Finally, suggestions and conclusions are incorporated in the chapter.

The second section of the book deals with the socio-cultural changes associated with globalization. The process of globalization has made deep inroads into the Indian social life. Globalization appears to be the buzzword of 1990s, which has penetrated many academic debates just as post-modernism was the most fashionable and debatable topic of the 1980s. A wide and diverse range of social theorists are arguing that today's world is organized by accelerating globalization, which is strengthening the dominance of a world capitalist economic system, supplanting the primacy of the nation-state with trans-national corporations and organizations, and eroding local cultures and traditions through a global culture. Marxists, world systems theorists, functionalists, Weberians and other contemporary theorists are converging on the position that globalization is a distinguishing trend of the present moment.

Indeed globalization is one of the most hotly debated issues of the present era. For some, it is a cover concept for global capitalism and imperialism, and is accordingly condemned as another form of the imposition of the logic of capital and the market on ever more regions of the world and spheres of life. For others, it is the continuation of modernization and a force of progress, increased wealth, freedom, democracy and happiness. Its defenders present globalization as beneficial, generating fresh economic opportunities, political democratization, cultural diversity and the opening to an exciting new world. Its critics see globalization as harmful, bringing about increased domination and control by the wealthier developed nations over the poor underdeveloped countries, thus increasing the hegemony of the "haves" over the "have-nots". In addition, supplementing the negative view, globalization critics assert that globalization produces an undermining of the democracy, a cultural homogenization, and increased destruction of natural species and the environment. Some imagine the globalization project – whether viewed positively or negatively – as inevitable and beyond human control and intervention, whereas others view it as generating new conflicts and new spaces for struggle, distinguishing between globalization from above and globalization from below (Brecher et al., 2000).

In this context, it becomes imperative to understand the impact of globalization on various sections of population. So, this section deals with the changes associated with globalization and its impact on youth, women and the scheduled castes. This section too has four chapters.

The fifth chapter *Globalization, Technology and Changing Youth Culture in India: A Sociological Perspective* explores the diverse impact of technology on youth population in India. In a country like India where the entire population is steadily getting younger, we have found ourselves absorbed with the concerns and interests, the aspirations and frustrations of youth in whatever situation they find themselves. Changing social circumstances with the advent of technology have transformed the pattern of earlier relationships and disturbed the orderly progression of youth. With heightened consumerism, the youth's lure for western lifestyle is increasingly gaining ground. A question therefore arises whether the changing circumstances have led to the transformation of their world view or identity thereby creating a separate cultural pattern. The youths today are seeking a universal identity; they are a new kind of population, who are more resilient and adaptable than the elders, ready for change, and open to new ideas. In this context, it is not possible to speak with detachment of "youth" a rather minor problem apart. Contemporary youths are in a particularly strategic situation while trying to adjust themselves to the "multiple realities" of the post-modern world. With tremendous growth in youth's commitment to cosmopolitan values, and yet the hold of tradition, caste and religion remaining intact, a situation of cultural dilemma does exist. One natural result of this uncertainty and confusion is that there is an increasing concern about, interest in and a searching for sound or meaningful value approach which can hold its own in a post-modern world. In recent times, because of increasing confusion evident in educational, political and social thinking of youth, there is a need to handle the "crisis" which has engulfed the future torch-bearers of our country. So, the chapter tries to unravel the emerging cultural traits and values with regard to major social institutions such as family and marriage among the Indian youth under diversified social situations and cultural contexts.

The sixth chapter *Locating Indian Women in the Context of Cultural Globalization: Changes and Possibilities* explores the impact of technology on the cultural life of women in India. Though globalization has affected every sector of life across caste, class and gender, yet its impact has brought about innumerable changes in the social and cultural lives of women. In this context, the chapter makes an analytical attempt to understand the various repercussions of globalization on women in India. It becomes imperative to understand the impact of cultural globalization on such a significant section of the population who have also been the major propellers of the social change. Though many scholars argue that globalization has been detrimental to women due to growing structural gender inequalities, others find greater opportunities to challenge pre-existing patriarchal norms through the role models in a globalized era. Since globalization is opening up the Indian economy suddenly at a very high speed, without the required economic and social policies to provide the much required safety net, women who have been involved with production in the traditional ways have to cope with numerous problems and yet try to avail of the opportunities which an open economy promises. The chapter focuses on the issue of emancipation of women in a globalized world. With respect to cultural globalization, the various aspects of globalization have promoted growing contacts between different cultures, leading partly to a greater understanding and cooperation, and partly to the emergence of trans-national communities and hybrid identities. So, it becomes important to explore what kinds of identities are formed among women in a globalized era? The underlying assumption is that women have never received equal treatment of homogeneous category and, when united as gender, other factors such as class, ethnicity and religion have further divided them in terms of the age, ideology and sexual preferences. Moreover, in the cultural sphere, the impact of globalization on women has been associated with the destruction of their cultural identities. Even women are considered victims of the accelerating encroachment of a homogenized, westernized consumer culture. However, such views are from the proponents of anti-globalization. On the contrary, the chapter looks at the identity issue as a product of globalization.

The seventh chapter *Globalization and Social Exclusion: The Social Location of Scheduled Castes in Indian Society and the Need for Inclusion* is an attempt to study the socio-economic position of scheduled castes in India and the problems faced by them even after so many economic policy adoptions. It should however be pointed out that globalization is making inroads into all the aspects of human life in all the countries in the world. It is imperative to understand this process and study the nature of the impact on various communities. This impact can be seen even in the developed countries, which is social, economic, political, cultural and even moral in nature. Since globalization is truly universal in nature, it naturally involves competition and quality. No individual would escape from these. And, there is no point in avoiding these. Quality and competition are the watchwords in this age of globalization. Fortunately, the Indian society has all the potentialities of these two. Moreover, unlike the United Nations, the WTO expects the members to accept at present any one service to be thrown open to all the members in the world. Therefore, there is no alternative to competition. And without quality, competition would have no meaning. Here, the other processes of liberalization and privatization are going to play an important role. Therefore, it is necessary to bring about changes to cope up with the problems associated with LPG (Liberalization, Privatization and Globalization). India is a plural society having many sections based on religion, caste, class, etc. These sections have different types of impact at different levels. It will be academically unfair to think about the impact of globalization unilaterally. Different sections or groups in a heterogeneous society have different problems. Even after 60 years of independence various social groups are not empowered to face the challenge of competing equally. Even now they need the positive support of the welfare state. In view of this, what is necessary is to have a rational balance between empowerment of the weaker sections and the achievement of quality to face the competition.

The last chapter, *Youth, Religion and Globalization* locates contemporary youth and explore the various changes in their culture and religious values in the context of their identity formation. In a country like India where the majority of population is steadily getting younger, it becomes essential to explore the concerns and interests of this vast majority of population. Today's youth are quintessential inhabitants of post-modern and global life because they are the first generation to live integrated within the changing spheres of hyper-reality where new technology, media and culture are altering all aspects of life. The youth today are a new kind of population who are growing up in a diverse multi-cultural environment, more mature in nature and are easily adaptable to change than the older generation. In this context, the present chapter explores the various changes taking place in the religious life of the modern youth. An important dilemma in the lives of youth is whether they uphold the cultural values transmitted by various religious traditions or whether there is a complete abolition of such values. Much of the bewilderment of the young and uncertainty stems directly from a decline in religious belief and practices. So, the chapter uncovers the varied experiences of youth in a globalized world and also tries to understand the multiple changes in the cultural and religious lives of youth.

References

Albrow, Martin. *The Global Age*. Cambridge: Polity Press, 1996.

Arrighi, Giovanni. *The Long Twentieth Century*. London/New York: Verso, 1994.

Axford, Barie. *The Global System: Economics, Politics, and Culture*. New York: St. Martin's Press, 1995.

Axtmann, Roland, ed. *Globalization in European Context*. London: Cassells, 1998.

Best, S. and D. Kellner. *Postmodern Theory: Critical Interrogations*. New York: Guilford Press, 1991.

Brecher, Jeremy, Tim Costello and Brendan Smith. *Globalization from Below*. Boston, MA: South End Press, 2000.

Cvetkovich, Ann and Douglas Kellner. *Articulating the Global and the Local: Globalization and Cultural Studies*. Boulder, CO: Westview Press, 1997.

Featherstone, Mike, ed. *Global Culture: Nationalism, Globalization, and Modernity*. London: Sage, 1990.

Featherstone, Mike, Lash Scott and Robertson Roland, eds. *Global Modernities*. California: Sage, 1995.

Friedman, Thomas. *The Lexus and the Olive Tree*. New York: Farrar Straus Giroux, 1999.

Giddens, Anthony. *Consequences of Modernity*. Cambridge: Polity Press; Palo Alto, CA: Stanford University Press, 1990.

Gilroy, Paul. *The Black Atlantic: Modernity and Double Consciousness*. Cambridge, MA: Harvard University Press, 1993.

Grewal, Inderpal and Caren Kaplan, eds. *Scattered Hegemonies: Post Modernity and Transnational Feminist Practices*. Minneapolis, MN: University of Minnesota Press, 1994.

Hardt, Michael and Antonio Negri. *Empire*. Cambridge, MA: Harvard University Press, 2000.

Held, David, Anthony McGrew, David Goldblatt and Jonathan Perraton. *Global Transformations*. Cambridge: Polity Press; Palo Alto, CA: Stanford University Press, 1999.

Held, David. *Democracy and the Global Order*. Cambridge: Polity Press; Palo Alto, CA: Stanford University Press, 1995.

Hirst, Paul and Grahame Thompson. *Globalization in Question*. Cambridge: Polity Press, 1996.

Kellner, D. "Multiple Literacies and Critical Pedagogy in a Multicultural Society", *Educational Theory* 48, 1998: 103–22.

King, Anthony D., ed. *Culture, Globalization, and the World-System: Contemporary Conditions for the Representation of Identity*. Binghamton, NY: SUNY Art Department, 1991.

Lash, Scott and John Urry. *Economies of Signs and Space*. London: Sage, 1994.

Lechner, Frank J. and John Boli. *The Globalization Reader*. Malden, MA: Blackwell, 2000.

Robertson, Roland. *Globalization*. London: Sage, 1991.

Steger, Manfred. *Globalism: The New Market Ideology*. Lanham, MD: Rowman and Littlefield, 2002.

Stiglitz, Joseph E. *Globalization and its Discontents*. New York: Norton, 2002.

Wark, McKenzie. *Virtual Geography: Living with Global Media Events*. Bloomington and Indianapolis, IN: Indiana University Press, 1994.

Waters, M. *Globalization*. London: Routledge, 1995.

Part I

GLOBALIZATION AND ECONOMIC LIFE

1

Globalization, Structural Reforms and Its Impact on Indian Agriculture

Indu Upadhyay

India was one of the leading developing nations which pleaded for the inclusion of agriculture within the purview of the General Agreement on Tariff and Trade (GATT) since the very beginning of the Urugway Round of discussions in September 1986, since it was felt that the developing countries have a comparative advantage in agricultural production. The principle of comparative advantage is built on the basis of inter-country differences in costs and returns between different commodities, abstracting from taxes and subsidies influencing these costs and returns. Further, it was also hoped by the developing countries that bringing agriculture into the ambit of WTO would result in better market access for them, thereby facilitating the much celebrated trade as the engine of growth. However, the principle of comparative advantage requires that prices be determined by market forces and that there should be no barriers on trade.

If some rich countries because of their ability to subsidize agriculture can sell their produce at artificially lower prices and thus undercut the market for genuinely efficient or low-cost producers, then, the playing field is highly uneven, as the principle of comparative advantage is not followed. Similarly, if some countries are taxing or discriminating against agriculture by heavily protecting their industry and through over-valued exchange rates, as most developing countries have been doing till recently, then their competitiveness is eroded vis-à-vis countries which do not tax agriculture. In this case too, the principle of comparative advantage is denied free play. Moreover, the world – despite increasing interdependence and integration among countries – is highly heterogeneous with regard to the level of development. There are countries at an advanced stage of development in regard to the levels of infrastructure and technology achieved over a period of a few centuries. On the other hand, there are several countries which have only recently emerged from long periods of colonial rule. They have a long way to go before they can achieve a level of playing field vis-à-vis developed countries in regard to infrastructure, technology and skills. Such countries may need protection for some time in certain specific areas before they can trap and realize their potential so as to be in a position to compete with the advanced countries as trading partners on an equal footing.

It needs no emphasis that the performance of agriculture in India is important as the sector not only contributes to the overall growth of the economy but also provides employment and food security to majority of the population in the country. The Eleventh Five-Year Plan also indicates that agricultural development is an important component of inclusive growth approach. As mentioned earlier, structural reforms were introduced in India in a big way in 1991. The reforms were followed by India becoming a founder member of WTO in 1994. The structural reforms and obligations of WTO have positive and negative effects on the

Indian agriculture. In this context, this chapter provides an overview of issues and policies on two aspects, namely, impact of structural macro-policy reforms on agriculture and reforms needed in agriculture in order to benefit from overall economic reforms and cope with the emerging challenges in the post-reform era.

Structural Reforms and Agriculture

It should however be pointed out that the greater market opportunities afforded by globalization did not automatically translate into greater welfare for the resource-poor farmers in India. The growth rate of agriculture in India has been declining since many

Table 1.1

Comparison of Average Annual Growth Rate of GDP and Agriculture and Allied Activities

Plans	*Annual Average Growth Rate*	
	Overall GDP Growth Rate (in %)	*Agriculture and Allied Activities (in %)*
Seventh Plan (1985–90)	6.0	3.2
Annual Plan (1990–92)	3.4	1.3
Eighth Plan (1992–97)	6.7	4.7
Ninth Plan (1997–02)	5.5	2.1
Tenth Plan (2002–07)	7.6	2.3
2002–03	3.8	–7.2
2003–04	8.5	10.0
2004–05 (P)	7.5	0.0
2005–06 (Q)	9.0	6.0
2006–07 (A)	9.2	2.7

P: Provisional; Q: Quick Estimates; A: Advanced Estimate.

Note: Growth rate prior to 2001 is based on 1993–94 policies and from 2000–01 onwards is based on series at 1999–2000 prices.

Source: Economic Survey 2006–07, p. 159.

years. As shown in Table 1.1, the average annual growth rate of agriculture and allied activities was 3.2 per cent during the Seventh Plan which increased to 4.7 per cent in the Eighth Plan. The growth rate declined to 2.1 per cent in the Ninth Plan. The average annual growth rate was – 7.2 per cent in 2002–03 which declined to zero per cent in 2004–05. The growth rate came to 2.7 per cent in 2006–07. The resource-poor farmers have not been benefited from globalization not because they were marginalized as is generally believed, but they have been highly receptive to international technology transfers and also increased their participation in export markets. Trade liberalization provided them an opportunity to expand their production of remunerative export such as cotton by using modern technology in the form of hybrid seeds, fertilizers and pesticides, and in spite of this the state of Indian agriculture is not in a better position.

The structural reforms and policies introduced in India in 1991 initially focused on industry, tax reforms, foreign trade and investment, banking and capital markets. The economic reforms did not include any package specifically designed for agriculture. It was viewed that freeing agricultural markets and liberalizing external trade in agricultural commodities would provide price incentives leading to enhanced investment and output in that sector, while broader trade liberalization would shift inter-sectoral terms of trade in favour of agriculture (Balakrishnan, 2000).

As revealed earlier, the domestic and border policies affecting agriculture were not included in the early reform period. According to Landes and Gulati (2004)[1], the terms of trade between industry and agriculture were against agriculture in 1980 but after liberalization and with the inflow of modern technologies these were made in favour of agriculture. In 1994, import restrictions on cotton, oilseeds and sugar were liberalized but most of the agricultural commodities remained subject to import control. As the reform gained pace, an inflow of modern techniques and foreign exchange took place slowly and all the restrictions were lifted in 2001. Another significant development that happened during 2001 was the commercial introduction of genetically modified cotton seed and varieties by an MNC – Mona Santo.

On the positive side, the reforms have improved terms of trade for agriculture and opened up new opportunities such as benefits from trade and specialization, widening choices in new technology including biotechnology, increase in private investment in irrigation and marketing infrastructure such as storage and transport. It is viewed that protection to industry in the form of import substitution policies like tight import controls and high import duties have hurt agriculture till 1991. Disprotection to industry since 1991 is supposed to correct this bias and increase terms of trade for agriculture. "This would create a potentially more profitable agriculture, which would be able to bear the economic costs of technological modernization and expansion", said Dr Manmohan Singh, then Finance Minister, Government of India.

Table 1.2

Index of Terms of Trade between Agriculture and Non-agricultural Sector

Year	*Combined Index of Price Paid*	*Index of Price Received*	*Agriculture's Terms of Trade*
1981–82	61.9	54.9	88.7
1982–83	66.0	60.3	91.4
1983–84	70.1	64.2	91.6
1984–85	72.4	68.0	93.9
1985–86	75.2	70.4	93.6
1986–87	80.2	76.7	95.7
1987–88	88.3	86.0	97.4
1988–89	91.8	90.3	98.3
1989–90	98.1	97.5	99.4
1990–91	110.2	112.3	101.9
1991–92	123.8	130.8	105.6

Cont'd...

...Cont'd

1992–93	133.5	138.7	103.9
1993–94	146.1	151.4	103.6
1994–95	160.5	171.1	106.6
1995–96	173.7	182.9	105.3
1996–97	184.8	190.6	103.1
1997–98	194.9	205.9	105.6
1998–99	209.9	220.8	105.2
1999–2000	214.0	219.8	102.7
2000–01	223.0	225.0	100.9
2001–02	229.0	235.3	102.8
2002–03	239.3	247.9	103.6
2003–04	248.7	251.2	101.0
2004–05	257.5	258.2	100.3
2005–06	270.6	275.8	101.9
2006–07*	285.4	291.1	102.0

*Provisional, Directorate of Economics and Statistics, Ministry of Agriculture.

Source: Keynote paper on Agriculture, Structural Reforms and Agriculture: Issues and Policies, by S. Mahendra Dev, Chairman, CACP.

A look at the terms of trade (Table 1.2) in post-reform period shows that it was favourable to agriculture. Agriculture grew at a rate of 3.7 per cent per annum in the first six years of the reform period (1991–97). The terms of trade in agriculture improved during this period due to disprotection to industry, devaluation of rupee and increase in minimum support prices. The growth rate of agriculture started declining since mid-1990s. The terms of trade deteriorated during this period. As the restrictions were lifted, the terms of trade became more and more against agriculture as is evident in Table 1.2.

It is very interesting to note that while the government pushed heavily for border policies, input subsidies on fertilizers, power and irrigation remained largely unaffected. It needs no emphasis that with the introduction of genetically improved seeds the requirement of fertilizers increased which one can easily understand after viewing Table 1.3. Production of breeder seeds increased from 65,880 quintals in 2005–06 to 69,980 quintals in 2006–07. Similarly, while the production of foundation seeds increased from 7.4 lakh Q to 8 lakh Q during the same period, the distribution of certified quality seeds increased from 126.7 lakh Q to 149.63 lakh Q.

It should however be pointed out that on one hand it leads to increased production and on the other hand it leads to increased cost of production. One of the characteristics of HYV seeds is that they cannot be bred by farmers themselves. Since time immemorial Indian farmers have been storing a part of the production to be utilized as seeds. But, the circumstances have changed now and they have to depend on various MNCs for seeds which leads to increased cost of production.

Table 1.3

Production and Distribution of High Yielding Variety Seeds

Year	*Production of Breeder Seeds (in Q)*	*Production of Foundation Seeds (in lakh Q)*	*Distribution of Certified Quality Seeds (in lakh Q)*
2003–04	61,826	6.5	108.59
2004–05	66,460	6.9	113.10
2005–06	65,880	7.4	126.70
2006–07	69,980	8.0	149.63

Source: Economic Survey, 2006–07.

It needs no emphasis that in order to increase production for the ever-increasing population the cultivation should either be done intensively or extensively. Extensive cultivation means increasing the land under cultivation while intensive cultivation aims at increasing production by increasing the variable factors of production, namely, fertilizers, pesticides, insecticides, etc. Indians began intensive method of cultivation in 1966. Table 1.4 shows increasing use of fertilizers in India. Fertilizers are generally defined as “any material, organic or inorganic, natural or synthetic which supply one or more chemical elements required for plant growth".

Sixteen elements are essential for plant growth, of which nine are required in macro-quantities and seven in micro-quantities. They are carbon, oxygen, hydrogen, nitrogen, phosphorous, potassium, calcium, magnesium, sulphur, baron, chlorine, copper, iron, manganese, molybdenum, zinc, etc. Of the elements listed above, carbon, oxygen and hydrogen are supplied by air and water. Phosphorous, potassium and nitrogen are known as the primary nutrients. Magnesium, sulphur, baron, chlorine, copper are known as secondary nutrients, while the elements remaining are called macro-nutrients. Here, fertilizers stand for the chemicals that are required to provide primary nutrients, secondary nutrients and macro-nutrients.[2] It needs no emphasis that when we go on growing crops, fertility of the land goes on declining as the nutrients are being absorbed from the land by the crops for their growth. Therefore, in order to make the land more fertile, it is very essential to supply the nutrients again in the form of fertilizers to the land to make it more fertile.

Table 1.4

Consumption of Major Fertilizers

(lakh tonnes)

Fertilizers	*2001–02*	*2002–03*	*2003–04*	*2004–05*	*2005–06*
Urea	199.17	184.93	197.67	206.65	222.97
DAP	61.81	54.73	56.24	62.36	67.64
MOP	19.93	19.21	18.41	24.06	27.31
Nitrogenous Fertilizers (N)	113.1	104.79	110.77	117.13	127.23
Phosphatic Fertilizers (P)	43.82	40.19	41.19	46.24	52.04
Potassic Fertilizers (K)	16.67	16.01	15.98	20.61	24.13
N+P+K	173.60	160.94	167.99	183.98	203.40
Percentage increase	3.94	–7.29	4.38	10.56	8.84

Source: Economic Survey, 2006–07.

The consumption of fertilizers increased from 173.60 lakh tonnes in 2001–02 to 183.98 lakh tonnes in 2004–05. It further increased to 203.4 lakh tonnes in 2005–06. One thing that should be mentioned here is that on one hand the production of the food grains is also increasing due to the application of heavy doses of fertilizers, on the other hand, the productivity and cost of production for the farmers is also increasing. The other thing which is important is the ratio at which the three fertilizers, namely, NPK, should be applied. Mostly it differs according to the type of soil. The ideal ratio for Indian soil is 4:2:1, i.e., if 4 kg of nitrogenous fertilizers is applied, 2 kg phosphorous and 1 kg of potassium should be also applied to get good results. Indian farmers have been using fertilizers different from this ratio. This can be shown in Table 1.5.

Table 1.5

Ratio of Consumption of Fertilizers

Year	*Nitrogen*	*Phosphorous*	*Potassium*
1955–56	10.8	1.3	1
1960–61	7.2	1.8	1
1980–81	5.9	1.9	1
1990–91	6.0	2.4	1
1998–99	8.3	3.0	1
2006–07	6.2	4.0	1

Source: Economic Survey, Government of India, Ministry of Finance, 1998–99, 2006–07.

The ratio of use of NPK was 10.8:1.3:1 in 1955–56 which became 6.0:2.4:1 in 1990–91. The ratio in 1998–99 was 8.3:3.0:1. Finally, in 2006–07, the ratio was 6.2:4.0:1 which is far away from the desirable ratio. It was felt by the steering committee of Planning Commission that since the nitrogenous fertilizers were subsidized more as compared to phosphatic and potassic fertilizers, they are used more as compared to potassic and phosphatic fertilizers (Economic Survey, 2007–08). In this regard, the government has changed its fertilizer policy to nutrient-based subsidy (NBS). Doubts have arisen about its success in achieving the twin objectives of reducing the fertilizer subsidy and remedying the imbalance in fertilizer use. The new policy has failed to improve price parity between urea and other fertilizers. As shown above, this is essential to ensure a balanced use of all the three nutrients, namely, NPK. The NBS system even while envisaging fixed subsidy linked to the nutrient content of different fertilizers also simultaneously decontrols the farmgate prices of fertilizers other than urea. Though the government has asked the fertilizer industry not to hike the prices of decontrolled fertilizers more than 5 to 6 per cent in the initial year of implementation of the NBS system, even this modest increase has upset the price mismatch between urea and other fertilizers, which is the root cause of higher application of N vis-à-vis P and K. While the 10 per cent hike in price of urea by the government (after keeping it constant at ₹ 4,800 per tonne since 2002) has meant an effective increase of only ₹ 480 per tonne, the prices of phosphatic and potassic fertilizers have gone up by over ₹ 600 to ₹ 700 per tonne and those of complex fertilizers containing even the micro-nutrients, such as sulphur, zinc, etc., by even a bigger margin. Thus, after the introduction of NBS, the disparity in the prices of different fertilizers has actually exacerbated. There is, therefore, little hope that the new system will adequately address the nutritional imbalance concerns.[3]

The other major input for Indian agriculture is the use of various pesticides such as fungicides, weedicides, rodenticides, etc. Use of pesticides increased after the adoption of Green Revolution in 1966. As the cropping pattern became more intensive the use of pesticides increased day by day. Consumption of insecticides in agriculture has increased more than 100 per cent from 1971 to 1994–95. For instance, insecticide consumption in India which was to the tune of 22,013 tonnes has increased to 51,755 tonnes by 1994–95 (www.indiastat.com) and the consumption of all these pesticides in the same period has increased more than two times, that is, from 24,305 tonnes to 61,357 tonnes (Indian Chemical Statistics, 2000–01). The consumption of pesticides, however, declined to 43,580 tonnes in

2000–01 and to 40,670 tonnes in 2004–05. In the year 2006–07, the consumption of pesticides declined to 37,950 tonnes (Economic Survey, 2007–08). In recent past, change has been observed in trends of pesticides consumption. As a consequence of adoption of Biointensive Integrated Pest Management Programme in various crops, the consumption of chemical pesticides (technical grade) has come down. The point to be noted is that the consumption pattern of pesticides in India is also different from the rest of the world.

In India, insecticides account for 76 per cent of the total domestic market while herbicides and fungicides have a significantly higher share in the global market. There are wide ranges of regional variations in consumption of pesticides in the country. In the year 2000–01, states such as Haryana, Punjab and Uttar Pradesh by consuming more than 5,000 MT (technical grade) pesticides annually ranked first in consumption of pesticides. Similarly, states like Andhra Pradesh, Gujarat, Karnataka, Kerala, Madhya Pradesh, Maharashtra, Rajasthan, Orissa and Tamil Nadu, which consumed between 1,000 and 5,000 MT, ranked second and states such as Assam, Bihar and Himachal Pradesh that consumed between 100 and 1,000 MT ranked third. States, such as Arunachal Pradesh, Jammu and Kashmir, Manipur, Mizoram, Nagaland, Tripura, Delhi and Union Territory of Pondicherry, which consumed pesticides between 10 and 100 MT annually, ranked fourth and states like Goa, Meghalaya, Sikkim and UTs, viz., Andaman and Nicobar Islands, Chandigarh, Dadra and Nagar Haveli, Daman and Diu, and Lakshadweep, which consumed less than 10 MT pesticides annually and fell in the last category in pesticide consumption (Thirty-Seventh Report of Standing Committee on Petroleum and Chemicals, 2002).

One of the consequences of such a huge use of pesticides in agriculture came in the form of the adverse health impact on the society in general and vulnerable populations such as children in particular. Some of the well-known health effects of pesticide exposure include acute poisoning, cancer, neurological effects and reproductive harm (CSE, 1997). In an empirical survey of some of the villages in Punjab, traces of DDT were found in breast milk which cause harmful effects on the health of not only the mothers but also on the infants for whom it is considered the safest mode of feeding without contamination. The major causes of concern in this respect are bio-accumulation of pesticides and the prolonged time period that they take to express the negative health consequences and ever-rising cost of production.

It should however be pointed out that the inability of the government to control agricultural subsidies has led to the deterioration of its capacity to invest in rural capital formation. The share of agricultural sector's capital formation in GDP declined from 2.2 per cent in the late 1990s to 1.9 per cent in 2005–06. This disturbing trend was partly due to the stagnation or fall in public investment in irrigation, particularly since mid-1990s. As the public investment in irrigation declined, there was increase in cost of production for the farmers, as after the initiation of economic reforms farmers of all categories (large, medium, small and marginal) invested in private wells. It should be emphasized here that digging wells is a large, lumpy and highly risky investment and the profitability of well ownership varies inversely with land ownership (Aggarwal, 2000). A World Bank (2001) survey of irrigation technologies in Andhra Pradesh in 1999–2000 found that even though small and marginal farmers accounted for around 80 per cent of the total holdings, they owned only 48 per cent of the electric-powered wells in the state.

One of the causes of increasing cost of production is the change in the pattern of production by farmers themselves. It should however be pointed out that after the lifting of restrictions on cotton in 1994 its prices increased immensely. This sharp increase in prices made cotton an attractive crop. In a study based on a panel data from 13 states, Kanwar and Sadoulet (2008) found that the area under cotton is highly responsive to gross profitability with the associated long run elasticity of 0.2 per cent which was higher than that for other cash crops. It should however be pointed out that India has the largest area in the world under cotton cultivation (21% of the total), but accounts for only 14 per cent of the global production. Compared to global levels the cotton yield in India is the lowest, mainly due to the poor quality of seeds, lack of irrigation, limited supply of quality seeds and poor management services. Marketing of cotton is done by three sources, viz., private traders, state-level co-operatives and Cotton Corporation of India (CCI), of which 70 per cent is done by private traders followed by state co-operatives and CCI. Minimum Support Price (MSP) is being regulated by Commission for Agricultural Cost and Prices for the past few years, the Government of Andhra Pradesh had been recommending higher MSP for cotton because of higher cost of production to the all-India average (GoAP, 2005). However, the union government did not follow these recommendations, and according to various studies the MSP is lower than the average cost of production (GoAP, 2005; NCF, 2006).

Table 1.6

Trend Growth Rate in Area, Input Use, Credit and Capita Stock in Agriculture during 1980 to 2005–06

(in %)

	1980–81 to 1990–91	*1990–91 to 1996–97*	*1996–97 to 2005–06*
Technology	3.3	2.8	0.
Public Investment	3.9	1.9	1.4
Private Investment	0.6	2.2	1.2
Irrigated Area	2.3	2.6	0.6
Area under Fruits and Vegetables	5.6	5.6	2.7
NPK Use	8.2	2.5	2.3
Credit	3.7	7.5	14.4

Source: Government of India, 2007; Keynote Paper on Agriculture, by S. Mahendra Dev, Chairman, CACP.

With the changing cropping pattern from the staple food crops to cash crops, the agriculture has become highly intensive in case of the use of purchased inputs leading to a sharp increase in the working capital requirements of the farmers. At all-India level, although cotton is grown on about 5 per cent of the cultivated area only, it accounts for 50 per cent of pesticide consumption (Venugopalan et al., 2004). The per hectare variable cost for unirrigated cotton cultivation in Warrangal district in 1997–98 was almost four times that for maize and 2.5 times for groundnuts. The sharp cost escalation led to increased indebtness of farmers (NSSO, 2005b). The survey reports pointed out that almost 82 per cent of the farm households in Andhra Pradesh (where mostly cash crops are grown) were indebted in comparison to only 49 per cent at all-India level.

It needs no emphasis that it was expected that after the adoption of structural reforms the old and outdated techniques will be substituted by cost and time efficient new techniques. Table 1.6 shows that the growth rate of technology was 3.3 per cent between 1980–81 and 1990–91 (pre-reform period), which declined to 2.8 per cent during 1990–91 to 1996–97 and further to nil during 1996–97 to 2005–06 (post-reform period). In case of public investment, the growth rate in the pre-reform period was 3.9 per cent which declined to 1.4 per cent after the adoption of reforms. In spite of the adoption of reforms the subsidies given to the agricultural sector were not reduced to the extent to which they should have been, therefore, the capacity of the government got reduced which is evident from Table 1.6. As the public investment declined, the burden on the private sector increased. The growth rate of private investment was 0.6 per cent in pre-reform era which increased to 1.2 per cent in post-reform period. The growth rate of the irrigated area during 1980–81 to 1990–91 was 2.3 per cent which declined to 0.6 per cent between 1996–97 and 2005–06. As the cost of production increased due to changes in Indian agriculture mentioned earlier in the chapter, the growth rate of credit also increased from 3.7 per cent during 1980–81 to 1990–91 to 14.4 per cent during 1996–97 to 2005–06 which was almost four times. It should however be pointed out that public spending on agricultural subsidies is crowding out productivity, and as India lacks roads, electricity, fertilizers and pesticides availability these cause vulnerable damage to the growth of agriculture.

Table 1.7 shows the gross capital formation in agriculture and allied activities as percentage of GDP. In the year 1999–2000, the public investment was 1.94 per cent which increased to 1.99 per cent in 2002–03, while private investment increased from 9.29 per cent to 10.69 per cent during the same period. Further, in 2007–08, the public investment was only 3.97 per cent while the private investment was 10.27 per cent. There is no doubt that public investment has increased after the structural reforms, still private investment plays a significant role in capital formation in the agricultural sector. Here, it is wrong to say that private investment gets induced due to increased public investment. In India, even though public share in capital formation has not increased as it should have been, still the private sector has continued to contribute more and more in the capital formation of this sector.

Table 1.7

Capital Formation in Agriculture and Allied Activities as Percentage of GDP

(in %)

Year	*Public Investment*	*Private Investment*	*Total Investment*
1999–2000	1.94	9.29	11.23
2000–01	1.81	8.40	10.21
2001–02	2.05	9.99	12.04
2002–03	1.99	10.69	12.68
2003–04	2.24	8.85	11.09
2004–05	2.70	9.28	11.98
2005–06	3.12	9.81	12.93
2006–07	3.53	10.26	13.79
2007–08	3.97	10.27	14.24

Source: Ministry of Agriculture, Government of India; Keynote Address on Agriculture, Structural Reforms and Agriculture: Issues and Policies by S. Mahendra Dev.

Now, the question arises as to whether the increasing share of private sector in capital formation is due to increasing revenue earned or on account of the past savings of the farmers. The point to be noted here is that the MSP has not been changed for years and therefore there is no question of increasing revenue. Cost of production has also been increasing on account of scientific and technical changes. Most of the money invested in capital formation comes from borrowing.

It should however be noted that most of the loans taken were expended on day-to-day expenses rather than capital expenses. It is really shocking, and has become a matter of concern. Several studies undertaken reveal that in spite of the expansion of the banking sector in rural area, a large section of the population remains outside the fold of formal credit institutions.

Table 1.8

Agency-wise Ground Level Credit Flow for Agriculture and Allied Activities

(in %)

Agency	*2002–03*	*2003–04*	*2004–05*	*2005–06*	*2006–07*
Co-operative Bank	23,716	26,959	31,424	39,404	33,174
RRBs	6,070	7,581	12,404	15,223	15,170
Commercial Banks	39,774	52,441	81,481	25,59	100,999
Total	69,560	86,981	1,28,308	1,80,986	1,49,343

Source: Economic Survey, 2006–07.

We can easily understand after analysing the data in Table 1.8 that the credit created in rural areas by the rural banks is increasing year by year. But, the thing that is really terrifying is that about 56 per cent of the farmers do not wish to have access to institutional credit and they remain dependent on non-institutional sources to fulfil their credit requirements, such as *Sahukars* and *Mahajans* and family members and relatives. Now, the question arises that at what rate of interest are the farmers getting this money? The interest rates on loans from non-formal sector, such as village moneylenders and traders, are significantly higher than those from formal sources. The interest rate in the institutional sector (banks) is 12 per cent for farmers while it is 36 per cent and above in case of non-institutional sources. So, it leads to a higher cost of production for the farmers. The most horrifying fact is that more than 50 per cent of the farmers are in the net of non-institutional sources of finance. Due to the increasing cost of production and lower revenue (as the MSP of many agricultural commodities has not been revised for years), the farmers are not able to pay back their liabilities so they either commit suicide or give up their profession and become petty workers in the industries of the nearby towns. This is something that is diverting agriculture from the path of sustainability. It needs no emphasis that in case of laws of variable proportion, keeping the fixed factor constant and the variable factor increasing to increase production, the production starts diminishing after a point. It seems that this is the reason behind diminishing returns in Indian agriculture in spite of addition of fertilizers, pesticides and insecticides. So, this is the correct time to start the Second Green Revolution, at least minimizing the use of chemical fertilizers and pesticides and using bio-fertilizers and pesticides instead. In an empirical survey, it was found that the intake of pesticides is more in the forms of food grains rather than having soft drinks such as Pepsi. Therefore, it is in broader national interest that the government should increase investment in rural infrastructure and encourage the use of bio-fertilizers and other nutrients which are essential for sustainable development of agriculture.

Conclusion

This chapter provides an overview of the issues and policies, the impact of structural macro-policy reforms on agriculture and reforms relating to supply-side factor in the agriculture sector. Conclusions drawn from the study indicate that structural reforms in agriculture have both positive and negative effects.

Agriculture got benefited indirectly due to overprotection given to industry in post-reform period. The terms of trade, private investment, opportunities for technology and specialization have increased for agriculture. On the negative side, trade reforms might have affected some crops and increased the dependence on global prices which are volatile. Fiscal and financial liberalization also had some adverse impact on the investments and credit. It has been concluded by some that the slowdown in Indian agriculture is linked directly to structural reforms[4] and globalization, including joining of WTO.

It may be further noted that the slowing in agricultural growth could be attributed to the structural factors on the supply side such as public investment, credit, technology, land and water management, fertilizer policy, etc., rather than globalization and trade reform per se. There are some deficit areas in the Indian agriculture. These are investment, credit and infrastructure deficit, laid water management deficit, research and extension (technology) deficit, diversification deficit, etc. Reforms are needed to reduce these deficits in order to achieve the goals of agriculture, i.e., 4 per cent growth in agriculture, equity in terms of higher growth in lagging reasons, small and marginal farmers and women, and sustainability.

Apart from high growth, efficiency (cost reduction) is also needed in the globalized world. Group approach among farmers should be encouraged in order to get inputs at cheaper rates and marketing of output at higher prices. There should be diversification of Indian diets away from food grains to high value products such as milk and meat products, and vegetables and fruits. Since risk is high for diversification, necessary support in infrastructure and marketing is needed. Price policy should also encourage diversification. The government is planning to have a Second Green Revolution by diversifying agriculture in crop sector and allied activities. To promote a holistic growth of horticulture sector through area-based regionally differentiated strategies, the National Horticulture Mission has been launched in the country during the 10th Plan. The impact has to be strengthened further to improve productivity in the horticulture sector. The true benefit of diversification will come if more emphasis is given to allied activities such as animal husbandry and fisheries. The livestock contributes 5.4 per cent to GDP and 22.7 per cent to the total output from the agricultural sector. Ownership of livestock is more equitable than that of land, and women play a significant role in animal husbandry.

The medium and long-term measures relating to supply side can also improve drought-proofing and de-risking agriculture. Similarly, rural non-farm sector has also to be developed. In spite of these measures, agriculture would always be subjected to shocks in the form of volatility in global agricultural prices and natural calamities such as droughts, floods and climate changes. Therefore, there is need to put in place social protection programmes and drought or flood management practices, including crop insurance, to take risks or shocks in agriculture. For example, social protection programmes such as PDS and rural public works programmes helped in a big way to overcome the drought effects in Gujarat and Rajasthan in 1987–88.

"Business as usual approach" may not help the revival of agriculture. A big push on the supply side is required for the promotion of agriculture. Similarly, demand factors also need to be stressed on. The government should address all the short-term and long-term problems in agriculture and should give a large push to core issues to make cultivation viable and profitable. There is also need to concentrate on the delivery system. India's large number of farmers can be benefited only if there are right policies and effective implementation.

It should however be pointed out that acceleration of growth of agriculture sector will not only push the overall GDP growth upwards, but it would also make it more inclusive and biased in favour of women. Increasing farm incomes is also necessary for an equitable growth. Further, with uncertainties in the global markets and hardening of international prices of food, fuels and edible oils, domestic price stability and food security critically depend on the growth in this sector. This necessitates working out forward and backward linkages that enhance productivity through balanced allocation and better utilization of available resources at all levels of implementation and quantifying output per unit of resources used. The issue of productivity and resource use assumes importance as agriculture continues to support more than half of the total population.

Notes

1. Landes and Gulati point out that budgetary outlays on major inputs have not been subjected to discipline under URAA. The subsidy outlays are below the minus levels, permitted in URAA and at any rate, each of the major subsidies has been notified as a subsidy for low-income and resource-poor farmers and hence not subjected to the discipline, 2004.
2. http://fert.nic.in/aboutfert/aboutfertilizers-asp
3. Reported in *Business Standard,* Vol. IV, No. 271, 22 April 2010.
4. Keynote Address on Agriculture, IEA, 2009.

References

Aggarwal, R.M. "Resource Poor Farmers in South India: On the Margins or Frontiers of Globalization", World Institute for Development Economics Research, 2006.

——. "Possibilities and Limitations to Cooperation in Small Groups: The Case of Group-Owned Wells in Southern India", *World Development* 28 (8), 2000: 1481–97.

Balakrishnan, P. "Agriculture and Economic Reforms: Growth and Welfare", *Economic and Political Weekly* 35 (12), 2000: 999–1004.

Centre for Science and Environment, New Delhi, 1997.

Centre for Science and Environment, New Delhi, 1998.

Economic Survey, Government of India, Ministry of Finance, Department of Economic Affairs, Economic Division, 2006–07.

Economic Survey, Government of India, Ministry of Finance, Department of Economic Affairs, Economic Division, 2007–08.

Government of Andhra Pradesh, 15th Report of Standing Committee on Chemicals and Fertilizers, Ministry of Chemicals and Fertilizers, 2005.

Government of Andhra Pradesh, Report of Commission on Farmers' Welfare, Department of Agriculture, Hyderabad, 2005.

Indian Chemical Statistics, Government of India, Ministry of Chemicals and Fertilizers, New Delhi, 2000–01.

Kanwar, Sunil and Elisabeth Sadoulet. "Dynamic Output Response Revisited: The Indian Cash Crops", *The Developing Economies* 46 (3), 2008: 217–41.

Landes, Rip and Ashok Gulati. "Farm Sector Performance and Reform Agenda", *Economic and Political Weekly* 39 (32): August 2004.

National Sample Survey Organisation, Ministry of Statistics and Programme Implementation, Government of India, New Delhi, 2005b.

NCF (Northwest Certified Forestry), (nnrgdb.org/news/documents/NCFFall2006Newsletter.pdf), 2006.

Singh, Manmohan. "Inaugural Address" delivered at 54th Annual Conference of Indian Society of Agricultural Economics held at Shivaji University, Kolhapur (Maharashtra) on 26 November 1994 and published in *Indian Journal of Agricultural Economics* 50 (1): January–March 1995.

Thirty-Seventh Report of Standing Committee on Petroleum and Chemicals, Ministry of Chemicals and Fertilizers (Department of Chemicals and Fertilizers), New Delhi, 2002.

Venugopalan, M.V., P. Chandran, D.K. Pal, O. Challa and S.L. Durge. "Effects of Organic and Conventional Cotton Production System on Soil Properties: A Case Study in Yavatmal district, Maharashtra", International Symposium on Strategies for Cotton Production, University of Agricultural Sciences, Dharwad, Karnataka, 2004, 118–21.

2

Food Security and Globalization in India

Indu Upadhyay

Three fundamental basic needs of humanity are food, shelter and clothing. Rightly does the Indian Constitution provide that every man, woman and child has right to food, to work and to enjoy the basic necessities such as education, medical aid and employment facilities. Unfortunately, even after 62 years of independence, the problem of food remains unsolved. It has been estimated that every third person in Asia suffers from hunger and a much larger people from malnutrition.

India is no exception to this observation. It should however be pointed out that Rome Declaration on World Food Security defines access to food as "physical and economic access, at all times, to sufficient, safe and nutritious food (for people) to meet their dietary needs and food preferences for an active and healthy life".[1] In other words, food security refers to security which requires access to adequate quantity and satisfactory quality of food. India has miserably failed in ensuring access to food for all our people. It should be noted that according to the National Family Health Survey conducted in 1998–99 at all-India level, 45.5 per cent of the children between the age of 6 and 36 months were stunted (undernourished on the basis of height), 47 per cent were undernourished, 74.3 per cent of the children of the same age group had anaemia and 51.8 per cent of all the women surveyed were anaemic.

Further in this regard, the National Nutrition Monitoring Bureau reports similar findings. Body Mass Index (BMI) was taken as an indicator of undernutrition in a study of eight states in 1991–92 wherein it was estimated that 46 per cent of men and women adults were energy deficient.

It needs no emphasis that India adopted New Economic Policy in the year 1991. These include the structural changes which deregulate, liberalize, and decontrol the various sectors of economy. The process of decontrolling leads to a change from Nehruvian socialism towards a new market economy. This standardized package of neo-liberal economic policy included devaluation of currency, privatization of efficient public enterprise, reduction of various subsides and liberalization of trade. No doubt it has brought about improvements in budgetary and fiscal conditions in some years – nevertheless such macro-economic changes on certain sectors such as agriculture were negative. It should however be pointed out that the present chapter is an attempt to look into the effects of the New Economic Policy on agriculture.

The study is mainly based on the secondary source of information. The data have been collected from Reserve Bank of India Bulletin, Currency and Finance Report, Reports of Planning Commission, Economic Survey, etc. Further, the study is divided into three sections: While the section deals with the historical evolution of the food problem and the requirement of food subsidy in Indian economy, the second section deals with the balance between demand and supply for agricultural commodities in the country. The last section presents conclusions of the study. In a nutshell, the objective is to study about the requirement of food security in India and to examine whether the supply is on a par with the demand for agricultural commodities in the country.

I

Malnutrition, starvation and occasional famines have been more or less endemic under Indian conditions.[2] "During the last 300 years, India has experienced 26 major famines: during the last 700 years there have been 17 very severe food disasters and during the historical time of the 34 great famines of the world 18 have occurred in India. The frequency and cyclical order show the peculiar susceptibility of this country to crop failures and recurrent shortage of food supply."[3]

It needs no emphasis that in the earlier part of the 19th century, India was a self-sufficient country in matters of food production, but in 1880, the Famine Commission sounded a note of warning that the pressure of the population was increasing on land. It pointed out that the country taken as a whole was definitely surplus in food, but the minority numbers opined that the alleged surplus (of 5 million tonnes) was greatly over estimated.[4] It should however be pointed out that food was not a problem for India at that time. Even in the years 1896–97 and 1899–1900 when there were famines, India exported 1.5 and 2.2 million tonnes of food grains, respectively. Even in the year 1921 when population started rising rapidly, the balance between demand and supply was maintained by increasing production of food grains.[5]

The position deteriorated after the separation of Burma in 1937, which was further aggravated with the outbreak of the Second World War as is clear from Table 2.1 showing the net production, imports and availability of food grains in India. In the year 1951, the net production was worth 48.1 million tonnes which was less than the requirement of the Indian economy. Therefore, 4.8 million tonnes had to be imported from various countries. The net production increased by 67.5 million tonnes in 1960 but still the imports of food grains were worth 5.1 million tonnes. The point to be noted is that even the imported food grain was not equal to the required quantity to satisfy the hunger. In this regard, the Agricultural Team (1959) observed: "An immediate and drastic increase in food production is India's primary problem of next 7 years. Without enough food India's hope for improving human welfare achieving social justice and securing democracy will become almost impossible of attainment."[6]

Table 2.1

Net Production, Imports and Availability of Food Grains (in million tonnes)

Year	*Net Production*	*Imports*	*Availability of Food Grains*
1951	48.1	4.8	52.4
1955	61.9	0.5	63.2
1960	67.5	5.1	71.2
1965	78.2	7.4	84.6
1970	87.1	3.6	89.5
1975	87.4	7.5	89.3
1980	96.0	–0.3	101.4
1985	127.4	–0.4	124.3
1990	149.7	1.3	144.8
1995	167.6	0.4	169.8
1996	157.9	–1.2	165.2
1997	174.4	1.0	177.2
2000	182.8	–1.4	155.8
2001	171.8	–2.9	146.5

Source: Economic Survey 2001–02, Ministry of Finance, Economic Division.

The team estimated that the country's demand for food was falling short by 28 million tonnes of food, but only 10.3 million tonnes could be imported. It needs no emphasis that the supply of food grains could not be increased, while the demand was increasing on account of the increasing population, rising income and defence expenditure. This caused a wide gap which had to be filled up by larger imports, intensification of internal procurement, taking over greater responsibility for distribution of available supplies by extension of rationing and opening of fair price shops, and launching emergency food production drive to encourage production of food grains. The imports rose sharply to 7.5 million in 1975. In 1980, the import of food grains was less than the exports, by –0.3 million tonnes. Further, in the year 1990 it was 1.3 million tonnes. Finally, in the year 2001, it became –2.9 million tonnes.

There is no denying the fact that food grain production has increased substantially in India. As a result in normal condition, there in no need to import food grains but still there are food deficit areas in India where supply of food grains does not match its demand. Therefore, providing minimum nutritional support to the poor through subsidized food grains and ensuring price stability in different states are the twin objectives of the food security system.[7]

II

It should however be pointed out that poverty in any state can be regarded as an indicator of need towards food security in that particular state.

Table 2.2 shows that the poverty was 55.72 per cent and 47.96 per cent in 1973–74 in rural and urban areas, respectively. In the year 1983, poverty stood at 45.31 and 35.65 per cent. Further in 1989–90 it was 39.06 and 36.60 per cent, respectively. In 1992, it stood at 43.47 and 33.73 per cent, respectively. In 1997, it was 35.78 and 29.99 per cent according to Datta's and S.P. Gupta's estimates (cited in NSSO 55th Round) and shows the same trend. In the year 1998, 43.01 per cent people lived under the poverty line of which 45.25 per cent were from rural areas, while 34.58 per cent were from urban areas. That means about 40 per cent of the people are not even able to fulfil their basic requirements after nearly two decades of adoption of economic reforms in India. Therefore, it is the responsibility of the government to provide them with the minimum nutritional standard which is not only important for their livelihood but also for efficient working of any economy. Therefore, food security is essentially required by any underdeveloped economy.

Table 2.2

Trends in Poverty: 1973–74 to 1998, All India

Year	*Datta's Estimates*		*S.P. Gupta's Estimates*		*Total*
	Rural	*Urban*	*Rural*	*Urban*	
1973–74	55.72	47.96	—	—	—
1977–78	50.60	40.50	—	—	—
1983	45.31	35.65	45.65	40.79	44.48
1986–87	38.81	34.29	—	—	—
1988–89	39.06	36.60	—	—	—
1989–90	34.30	33.40	33.70	36.00	34.28
1990–91	36.43	32.76	35.04	35.29	35.11
1991	37.42	33.23	—	—	—
1992	43.47	33.73	41.70	37.80	40.70
1993–94	36.66	30.51	37.27	32.36	35.07
1994–95	41.02	33.50	38.03	34.24	36.98
1995–96	37.15	28.04	38.29	30.05	36.08
1997	35.78	29.99	38.46	33.97	37.23
1998 (six months)	—	—	45.25	34.58	43.01

Source: Estimates based on NSS data on consumer expenditure.

Now, the question arises as to whether the Indian Government should continue to give food security or should gradually phase it out, as it is against the philosophy of globalization? It should however be pointed out that since India adopted New Economic Policy in 1991 the growth rate of the food subsidy has been uneven. This can be shown by Table 2.3.

Table 2.3

Growth of Food Subsidy in India (Other than Sugar)

Year	*Food Subsidy (in ₹ Crores)*	*Annual Growth (in %)*
1997–98	7,500	45.2
1998–99	87,00	16.0
1999–2000	9,200	5.8
2000–01	12,010	30.5
2001–02	17,494	45.7
2002–03	24,176	38.2
2003–04	25,160	4.1
2004–05	25,746	2.3
2005–06	23,071	–10.4
2006–07	23,828	3.3
2007–08 (BE)	25,425	6.7

Source: Economic Survey 2007–08, Government of India, Ministry of Finance, Economic Division.

Provision of minimum nutritional support to the poor through subsidized food grains and ensuring price stability in different states have been the twin objectives of the food security system in India. To fulfil the obligation towards distributive justice, the government incurs food subsidy. Table 2.3 shows that the food subsidy was ₹ 7,500 crores in 1997–98 when the average annual growth rate of food subsidy stood at 45.2 per cent. The quantum of food subsidy increased to ₹ 12,010 crores, while the annual growth was 30.5 per cent in 2000–01. Further, during the year 2003–04, the food subsidy increased in absolute terms and stood at ₹ 25,160 crores but the annual growth rate of subsidy declined to 4.1 per cent. In the year 2005–06, food subsidy declined to ₹ 23,071 crores and the annual growth rate of subsidy became negative by –10.4 per cent. Finally, in the year 2007–08, the food subsidy was ₹ 25,425 crores, while the growth rate of food subsidy stood at 6.7 per cent. Food subsidy showed an annual increase of 30 per cent during each of the three years 2000–01, 2001–02 and

2002–03, but has been relatively stable since 2003–04. It should however be pointed out that in a country where nearly 40 per cent people are not able to live with minimum nutritional standards required for living, it is the responsibility of the government to look after them. Therefore, food security is required to be continued.

It should however be pointed out that food subsidy being the difference between the economic cost of wheat and rice and their issue price, the quantum of food subsidy for different groups of beneficiaries is to be linked to the increase in economic cost and the issue prices. However, the economic cost of wheat has gone up due to an increase in the minimum support price (MSP), the issue price has been kept unchanged since July 2002[8] as can be shown by Table 2.4.

Table 2.4

MSP and Issue Price for Wheat and Rice Under TPDS

Marketing Season	*Minimum Support Price*		*Central Issue Price*					
	Wheat	*Paddy*	*Wheat*			*Rice*		
			APL	*BPL*	*AAY*	*APL*	*BPL*	*AAY*
2002–03	620	550	610	415	200	795	565	300
2003–04	630	550	610	415	200	795	565	300
2004–05	630	560	610	415	200	795	565	300
2005–06	640	570	610	415	200	795	565	300
2006–07	700	620	610	415	200	795	565	300
2007–08	850	745	610	415	200	795	565	300
2008–09	1,000	—	—	—	—	—	—	—

Notes: From 1 April 2002 to 30 June 2002, the issue price for APL for both wheat and rice was reduced by ₹ 100 per quintal.
MSP and CIP (for APL families) for Paddy/rice are for common grade.

Source: Government of India, Ministry of finance, Economic Survey 2007–08, p. 179.

Table 2.4 shows that the MSP has continued to rise since 2002. It was ₹ 620 for wheat and ₹ 550 for Paddy, while the issue price was ₹ 610, 415, 200 for wheat and ₹ 795, 565, 300 for rice for APL, BPL and AAY, respectively, in the year 2002–03. Further, in the year 2005–06, the MSP of wheat increased to ₹ 640, while the issue price remained the same at ₹ 610, 415, 200 for APL, BPL and AAY, respectively. Similarly, in 2007–08, the MSP of wheat increased and stood at ₹ 850, while the issue price remained the same at ₹ 610, 415 and 200, respectively. The point to be noted is that in order to maintain a minimum standard of nutrition, the Government of India has kept issue price as it is since 2002–03, which has resulted in an increase in the burden of food subsidy for the government. It needs no emphasis that the issue price is different for the three segments below poverty line (BPL), above poverty line (APL) and Antyodaya Anna Yojana (AAY). People who are above poverty line do not require food subsidy as they are able to pay for what they consume. But the point to be noted is that the MSP at which the food grains are available in the open market is always more than issue price for the same category of people for the same commodity leading to an increased burden of food subsidy.

While the total amount of subsidy has continued to rise in absolute terms, the state-wise allocation of subsidies is not related to poverty levels. The ratio of the percentage allocation of subsidies does not seem to correspond to the poverty levels. The ratio of percentage allocation of subsidies as given by the off take of food grains under TPDS and the proportion of people below poverty line is less than one for many of the poorer states as shown in Table 2.5.

Table 2.5 shows that Uttar Pradesh, the most populous state of India, where 19.6 per cent people are not able to fulfil their bare necessities, only 0.8 per cent people of the state are benefited by the food security. Second in the ladder is Bihar where 12.2 per cent people live below the poverty line but only 0.3 per cent people enjoy the benefits of food security. Third in the ladder is Maharashtra where 10.5 per cent people live below the poverty line while only 0.8 per cent people get its benefits. Fourth one is Madhya Pradesh where 8.3 per cent people live below the poverty line of which only 0.7 per cent enjoy the benefits of food subsidy.

Table 2.5

Allocation of Subsidies and Population Below the Poverty Line

State	*Food Subsidy for TPDS*			*% of Total Food Subsidy*	*% of People Below Poverty Line*	*Ratio of % of Subsidies to % of Persons Below Poverty Line*
	2005–06 (₹ Crores)	*2006–07 (₹ Crores)*	*Average*			
Bihar	975.1	625.1	800.1	3.5	12.2	0.3
Punjab	119.2	49.6	84.4	0.4	0.7	0.5
Jharkhand	678.1	429.4	553.7	2.4	3.9	0.6
Rajasthan	882.4	388.5	635.4	2.8	4.5	0.6
Madhya Pradesh	1571.4	949.0	1260.2	5.5	8.3	0.7
Uttar Pradesh	4024.3	2766.3	3395.3	14.8	19.6	0.8
Maharashtra	2183.5	1499.6	1841.6	8.0	10.5	0.8
Haryana	275.0	139.1	207.1	0.9	1.1	0.9
Orissa	1111.8	1130.9	1121.4	4.9	5.9	0.8
Gujarat	744.4	438.7	591.6	2.6	3.0	0.9
Goa	18.6	18.3	13.5	0.1	0.1	1.0
Chhattisgarh	787.9	663.4	725.7	3.2	3.0	1.1
West Bengal	1903.2	1593.4	1748.3	7.6	6.9	1.1
Karnataka	1611.9	1409.0	1510.5	6.6	4.6	1.4
Delhi	373.0	239.4	306.2	1.3	0.8	1.8
Kerala	821.6	674.7	748.1	3.3	1.6	2.0
Tamil Nadu	2636.1	2595.2	2615.7	11.4	4.8	2.4
Andhra Pradesh	2415.3	2243.0	2329.1	10.2	4.2	2.4
Total of All States	25813	19945.5	22.8	79.3	100	—

Notes: 1. Subsidies have been calculated on the basis of off take and difference between economic cost and issue price.
2. Share of BPL population is per Planning Commission 2004–05.
3. Total covers all the states and UTs including the ones not specifically mentioned.

Source: Government of India, Ministry of Finance, Economic Survey 2007–08, p. 180.

Now, let us take a glance of the relatively better-off states such as Goa, where only 0.1 per cent people live below the poverty line but 1.0 per cent people avail the benefits of the public distribution system (PDS). The next richer state is Delhi where only 0.8 per cent people live below the poverty line while 1.8 per cent people avail the benefits of the PDS. Third in order is Punjab where 0.7 per cent people live below the poverty line while 0.5 per cent people enjoy the benefits of food security. It should however be pointed out that for people who are not able to fulfil even their basic requirements the government should spend for them. However, the situation here appears to be quite different because the states having lower per capita income, where relatively more people live below the poverty line as compared to the richer states and still they avail relatively less benefits of cheaper food grains being provided under PDS. On the other hand, the richer states where per capita income is higher as compared to their underdeveloped counterparts take the benefits of food security more even though their citizens can bear the entire cost, i.e., MSP. One of the causes of this may be lack of food grains in the buffer stock available with the states. It is for this reason that in view of the declining stock position of the Central Pool, the Central Government has taken several steps to mitigate the shortage of wheat, such as rationalization of allocation of wheat for APL category under the TPDS and imports of wheat. The allocation of wheat under TPDS for APL category has been rationalized from June 2006 based on each state's average off take during the earlier three years or last year's off take, whichever was lower. A 25 per cent cut was imposed on rice-consuming states. However, there has been no change in the overall allocation entitlements for BPL and AAY category. The Department of Food and Public Distribution has released about 1 lakh tonnes of wheat under APL category for all the states/UTs every month from September 2006 to July 2007 and further from September 2007 to March 2008. Similarly, keeping in view the stock position of rice in the Central Pool, allocation of rice made for the APL category under the TPDS has been rationalized from April 2007 for all the states/UTs on the basis of their off take during 2003–04, 2004–05 and 2005–06. While the allocation for AAY and BPL categories is made at

35 kg/family per month, the allocation for APL category is made depending upon the availability of stocks in the Central Pool.

Patterns of Urban Consumption

Poverty is one of the major problems faced by the Indian economy, which can no doubt be solved by the PDS, but a new problem of obesity is cropping due to the changing pattern of consumption and even this problem can be solved by food security. As incomes go up, the food basket becomes more diversified. Cereal consumption decreases and the consumption of other foods increases. Even though people spend a smaller share of their income on food, they spend more in absolute terms. The urban food basket is the most diversified. Urban people consume fewer cereals and more of other items. Protective foods such as pulses, fruits and vegetables, milk, eggs and meat (including mutton) are easily available in the urban environment. If prosperity arising from economic growth and the influence of globalization was positive, then we could expect a more balanced diet away from cereals and towards protective high-protein foods, fruits and vegetables at the average level. In addition to the change in the consumption pattern over time at the all-India level, the study has also examined the consumption basket at the state level. Differences between prosperous states such as Delhi, Punjab and Haryana on the one hand and underprivileged states such as Orissa and Bihar on the other capture the impact of globalization on the consumption pattern.

Trends in Average Consumption

Data on the physical quantities of consumption of various items have been collected and published by the National Sample Survey Organization (2001a). For urban India as a whole from 1987 to 1988 and from 1999 to 2000, the consumption has changed. Consumption of rice and wheat has decreased marginally. Milk and egg consumption has recorded an increase. Substantial increases over the various time periods have been seen in the consumption of tea, biscuits, salted snacks, prepared sweets, edible oils, sugar and country sugar (jaggary). There is a decline in the intake of fruits and vegetables. Thus, it seems that diets have shifted towards more sugars and fats, lesser fruits and fewer vegetables. There is no evidence of a substantial shift of average diets towards nutritive and protective foods. The phenomenal growth in biscuit and tea consumption is more a result of prosperity and changing preferences. Therefore, the impact of globalization on these two items appears to be at best indirect (Table 2.6).

Table 2.6

Change in the Pattern of Consumption of Selected Food Items of the Urban Population (kg/month/per capita)

Food Items	*1987–88*	*1993–94*	*1999–2000*
Rice	5.26	5.13	5.10
Wheat and flour	4.37	4.44	4.45
Pulses	0.87	0.77	0.85
Liquid milk (l)	4.26	4.89	5.10
Eggs (in number)	1.23	1.48	2.06
Milk fat	0.04	0.05	0.07
Edible oils	0.41	0.46	0.74
Flesh food	0.39	0.40	0.46
Vegetables	3.94	3.09	3.00
Leafy vegetables	0.40	0.55	0.17
Mangoes	N.A.	0.12	0.16
Bananas (in number)	5.10	4.48	5.00
Lemons (in number)	N.A.	1.23	1.39
Sugar/Jaggary	0.97	0.97	1.32
Tea leaf	60.43	63.93	70.44
Salted refreshments	0.04	N.A.	1.36
Prepared refreshments	0.11	N.A.	0.40
Biscuits	0.07	N.A.	2.06

Source: GoI, National Sample Survey Organization, 2001a.

The pattern of consumption across the expenditure classes among the urban population reveals the same tendency. Per capita consumption of foods rich in protein such as pulses, milk products, eggs, fish and meat is far from adequate in all income classes. Consumption of pulses is barely above the Indian Council of Medical Research (ICMR) norm only in the highest three income classes, constituting about 20 per cent of the population. None of the expenditure groups consume adequate quantities of eggs, fish and meat. Forty per cent of the population consumes milk below the norm of 150 ml.

Consumption of foods such as fruits that provide vitamins and micro-nutrients is fairly low, even in the diets of the higher income classes. Fruit consumption is barely above the ICMR norm in any expenditure class, with the exception of the highest class, constituting 5 per cent of the population. Consequently, 95 per cent of the people have diets that are lacking in fruits. Vegetables are consumed in almost all expenditure classes (100–300 g/per capita/day). This would appear to be adequate. Part of the quantity consumed is in the form of tubers which are rich in carbohydrates, leaving the diets inadequate in green and yellow vegetables.

It is interesting to note that in urban areas consumption of processed foods and ready to eat foods has gone up together with income. The tendency is clear across all expenditure classes except in the lowest three classes, consisting of about 20 per cent of the population. Consumption of beverages, biscuits, processed foods, salted snacks, prepared sweets and other purchased foods constitutes 100–427 g/per capita/day, from the lowest to the highest expenditure class. Average consumption is about 167 g/per capita/day. This is probably an indication of the increasing consumption of snack foods and high-calorie foods such as sweets which are purchased away from the home. Energy-wise they may contribute to as many as 1,000 kcals in the daily diet, or 30 to 40 per cent of the required calories in the high-income classes.[9] It should however be pointed out that various transnationals have entered the domestic market, increasing investment and competition in the post-liberalization period. Some cocoa products, soft drinks, alcoholic beverages, and mineral and packaged water are also important in the consumer food industry. Soft drinks constitute a significant contribution as it is the third largest industry after packed tea and biscuits.

This has attracted the largest foreign direct investment in the country of over US$1 billion in recent years. Production was about 6.6 billion bottles in 2001–02 (Ministry of Food Processing Industries, GoI, 2003). Various transnationals have entered the domestic market, increasing investment and competition in the post-liberalization period. Some cocoa products, soft drinks, alcoholic beverages, and mineral and packaged water are also important in the consumer food industry. Soft drinks constitute a significant contribution as the third largest industry after packed tea and biscuits. Since liberalization in 1991, total investment in the processed food sector has been in the range of US$156 billion (of this, foreign direct investment has been about US$2 billion). Thus, urban consumption patterns are influenced by globalization across all expenditure groups except the lowest. Direct consumption of popular global brands on the one hand and the consumption of cheaper substitutes on the other have increased the overall consumption of processed foods (ibid.). It is noteworthy that the processing of meat, poultry, fish, eggs, milk, vegetables and fruit has not shown any significant increase. About 15 per cent of the milk and 2 per cent of fruits and vegetables are processed. Egg and poultry meat production increased from about 0.58 million tonnes in 1995 to 0.97 million tonnes in 2001 (ibid.). The food processing industry as well as urban consumption patterns are highly skewed towards cereal- and sugar-based products and not towards meat, fish, poultry, milk and vegetables. One of the causes behind this may be the ever-rising prices of the necessities, which can be seen from Table 2.7. As the necessities are beyond the reach of people therefore they prefer to purchase readymade fast-food. Many empirical surveys show that fast-foods lack nutritive value but have more calories than traditional Indian foods which leads to obesity in the Indian economy. The consumption of fizzy drinks, pizzas, potato crisps, etc., has increased in the diets of the urban population, as witnessed by the sales increase in these items. Undoubtedly, globalization has facilitated the entry of branded products and outlets into the market, such as Coca-Cola, Pepsi-Cola, Pizza Hut, Domino's Pizza and McDonald's, primarily for the more affluent consumers. Other local products of a cheaper variety, both by branded and unbranded producers, flood the markets. Globalization is the main cause of the expanding market for ready to eat foods. Although the branded product market is not very big, it is growing. For example, Amul is an established company producing milk powder and butter in India, however it has started competing with the global brands for cheese and pizza in recent years (Bhushan and Damodaran, 2001).

A number of unbranded producers flood the markets with cheaper products such as potato crisps and pizzas to woo consumers and suit the pockets of the lower-income groups. Domino's sells about 100,000 pizzas. Pizza Hut sells 40,000 pizzas and Amul sells about 50,000 frozen pizzas a day (Pizzamarketplace.com, 2003). The prices range anywhere from ₹ 20 for an Amul frozen pizza to ₹ 450 for a special premium large pizza from Domino's (ibid.). The unbranded market tends to be larger.

It has been found that for urban India as a whole and also for many states across the urban expenditure classes, cereal consumption has been declining since the 1970s. This trend is clear from the National Sample Surveys (NSS). The average urban Indian's per capita monthly consumption of cereals decreased from 11.36 kg in 1970–71 to 10.63 kg in 1993–94, and further to 10.42 kg in 1999–2000. In 1993–94, cereal consumption by the lowest 10 per cent was 9.51 kg per capita per month. It marginally increased to 9.55 kg in 1999–2000. However, despite this increase, the calorie intake of the lowest 10 per cent decreased over the same period, from 1,893 kcals per consumer unit to 1,889 kcals. Many others who have analysed the NSS data have also noticed the decreasing trend even for the lower expenditure classes (Radhakrishnan, 2002).

Decreases in the average cereal consumption are not of concern, as the average calorie intake of the urban population in all the states was found to be fairly high and above 2,100 calories, both in 1993–94 and in 1999–2000. Before the calorie data are analysed some explanations are in order. The consumption data for 1999–2000 have been alleged to be overestimated. However, what is striking is that despite this bias towards overestimation, the actual calorie intake of the lowest deciles in many states was quite low and below acceptable level (Swarna Sadasivam Vepa, 2003).

Some economists feel that the slowdown in cereal demand is a result of changes in the tastes and preferences of the people. Wherever infrastructure developments and prosperity related to globalization and imports make more of the other food items available, cereal consumption decreases. It is argued that this is not a sign of deterioration in human welfare (Rao, 2000). The demonstration effect and the availability of a variety of foods, some of which may be more nutritious than cereals, could be some of the reasons for an increase in the cost of calories consumed by the urban poor.

Another important point is that those consuming diets deficient in calories are not able to utilize other nutrients effectively since in the absence of sufficient calories, protein and other nutrients are not well utilized. Furthermore, many micro-nutrients are better absorbed by the body only if a balanced diet sufficient in calories is eaten. Varieties of foods that enhance the absorption of nutrients are ideal. For example, the absorption of iron improves if there are traces of Vitamin 'C' in food. Hence, the bottom line for better nutritional status is the minimum calorie intake per consumer unit. Sufficient calories should be consumed, and it is advantageous if they come from a variety of food items.

It needs no emphasis that overall the political and policy environment is clearly important in making the necessary commitment to strive for adequate health and nutrition of entire populations, both rural and urban, in any country. The provision of infrastructure, including roads and electricity, and education and healthcare systems, is a basic prerequisite to allow citizens to avail themselves of greater economic opportunities created through market liberalization and increased foreign investment. Greater individual economic prosperity fuels several household-level changes in lifestyles, including greater access to communications technologies, labour-saving devices and entertainment options. The synthesis demonstrates that access to these new technologies varies markedly from country to country and within countries, and certainly also between urban areas. In many instances, the forces at work are overloading the capacity of cities to accommodate the large and ever-increasing influx of people who are leaving the rural areas to migrate to the cities. A significant part of the reality underlying this phenomenon is that rural areas are no longer adequate livelihoods for the majority of populations. People move to cities because they are perceived to offer better "survival" opportunities. The forces of globalization affect the economic development and lifestyles in developing countries in a variety of ways. From a health and nutrition point of view, the most obvious changes are those resulting in sedentary lifestyles and adoption of dietary patterns that can lead to high rates of obesity and NCDs (non-communicable diseases). Despite some improvement, under nutrition and micronutrient deficiencies are generally still present. In other words, for the majority of cases, the issue of food and nutrition security has not been resolved, yet another level of complexity is being added to the problem as the incidence of diet-related NCDs increases.

The emergence of supermarkets and fast food chains, while catering to the changing demands of the consumer in terms of convenience, quality and safety, engenders new problems. These include erosion of food culture and reduction in biodiversity as a result of the newly created demand for standardized, uniform produce. Additionally, there has been a loss of livelihood opportunities at various stages of the food sector, including agricultural production.

Creating more equitable access to the new opportunities provided through globalization seems unlikely, at least in the short term, without very generous development assistance and a large dose of international good will, including fair access to world markets for agricultural products. A concerted effort to diminish inequalities and focus on delivering positive gains is needed to stem the tide of the increasing double burden of under nutrition and over nutrition coupled with excessive urbanization rates and growing poverty. The challenge for the global community to move smoothly towards a truly sustainable and inclusive "global village" has never been as great as it is at present.

III

It has been proved by researches that India had abundance of food for its citizen. But, after 1937, the food crisis started and in order to maintain the minimum nutritional requirement food subsidy was started. It should however be pointed out that efforts have been made by the Government of India to increase the net production of food grains since the planning started. No doubt that the production has increased by more than four times since the inception of the plan. Now, the question arises whether the balance between the demand and supply of food grains has been secured? It appears that the government has tried its best by importing food grains, maintaining buffer stock of food grains, providing food grains at lower prices to the people belonging to BPL, APL, etc. However, Table 2.2 shows somewhat different facts. According to S.P. Gupta's (1998) estimates, still 45.25 per cent people in rural areas, 34.58 per cent people in urban areas and a total of 43.01 per cent people live below the poverty line. That means near about half of the population of India is not able to provide itself with minimum nutritional standards.

There is no denying the fact that India adopted the philosophy of globalization in the year 1991 and were supposed to reduce subsidies of all kinds. Table 2.3 shows that India has given food subsidy to the extent of ₹ 25,428 crores in 2007–08 which was ₹ 23,825 crores in 2006–07. No doubt, the subsidy has increased in absolute terms, but the food subsidy which was 45.2 per cent in 1997–98 declined to 6.7 per cent in 2007–08. It is clear that India's expenditure or food subsidy bill has more than doubled from the year 1997 to 2008, but it should be noted that in a country where near about half of the population is not able to satisfy its hunger it is but natural that the government should support these people (BPL) through food subsidy.

It should however be pointed out that in Table 2.4 the MSP of wheat was ₹ 620 in 2002–03 which increased to ₹ 850 in 2007–08, while the issue price remained at ₹ 610, 415 and 200 for APL, BPL and AAY, respectively during the same period. Same is the case with rice where the MSP was ₹ 550 in 2002–03 which increased to ₹ 745 in 2007–08 for paddy, while the issue price remained at ₹ 795, 565 and 300 during the same period for APL, BPL and AAY, respectively. This is one of the causes regarding the increase in the government's burden of food subsidy in absolute terms.

Now, the question arises whether the food subsidy really helped in reducing the hunger of people below the poverty line. Table 2.5 shows that in Uttar Pradesh 19.6 per cent people live below the poverty line, while only 0.8 per cent people were covered by food security system. Next in terms of poverty ratio is Bihar where 12.2 per cent people were below the poverty line, while only 0.3 per cent people were benefited by the PDS. If we take the example of the richer states such as Goa, 0.1 per cent people were below the poverty line and 1 per cent people availed the benefits of food subsidy. In the case of Delhi, where 0.8 per cent people were below the poverty line, 1.8 per cent people enjoyed the food subsidy. That means in relatively poorer states, the PDS has failed to achieve its objectives because relatively lesser number of people are able to avail the benefits of PDS. There can be many reasons for this. This could be either because of institutional barriers, such as need to prove residence and buy ration entitlement once a fortnight. Migrant households do not satisfy the first requirement, while the poorest households do not have enough savings to buy in bulk. Apart from inadequate access to the PDS, there is the huge cost of providing subsidies to the poor through the PDS. Indeed many researches show that it costs more than a rupee of subsidy to the target families.[10]

It should however be pointed out that merely providing food grains such as wheat and rice is not sufficient for the poorer sections of the society. There is no denying the fact that a balanced diet is required which includes not only carbohydrates but also proteins, minerals, vitamins in the balanced quantity for healthy body, mind, etc. However, in an economy where prices are sky-rocketing, it is very difficult for the consumer, especially for those below the poverty line, to have balanced diet. Therefore, it is the duty of the state to provide other articles of consumption which are necessities as well.

Table 2.7

Comparative Analysis of Prices of Some Commodities

Name of Genes	*Prices (per kg/l)*	
	2004 (in ₹)	*2009 (in ₹)*
Wheat normal	8.50	11
Flour	9.00	13
Gram	20	32
Channa dal	25	40
Arhar dal	30	90
Rice	10	20–22
Mustard oil	55	65
Vanaspati ghee	50	60
Desi ghee	160	220–240
Besan	25	40–42
Sugar	18	28
Gur	16	28
Salt	6	12
Red chilly	65	70
Turmeric	40	100

Source: Reported in *Hindustan*, 17 July 2009.

As can be seen from Table 2.7, it is very difficult for a poorer family to take protein which is found in pulses which are ₹ 40/kg (Channa Dal) and ₹ 90/kg (Arhar Dal). It seems that oil and sugar which are the basic necessities are also out of their reach due to increasing prices. Therefore, other commodities which are not part of a balanced diet and at least are necessities for the people should be provided through the PDS at reasonable prices.

Even if the right to food is restricted to just food grains alone, the delivery mechanism will pose to be one of the biggest challenges for the government. The PDS has become something like a sacred cow and many people assert that the PDS is the only option before the government. However, this view completely ignores the shortcomings of the PDS as shown above.

An alternative to the PDS is the system of food stamps. Under this scheme, the government issues coupons to the target families. These coupons can then be redeemed at any shop – private or public for specified quantities of food grains at stipulated prices. Obviously, the government will have to pay the private retailer the difference between the stipulated price and market price.

The PDS and the system of food stamps can have the same level of leakages due to the targeting costs – the identification of BPL families must precede both systems. So, the effectiveness of food stamps obliviously depends on how efficient it is in delivering food grains to the consumers as compared to the PDS. By its very nature, food stamps do not have some of the costs associated with the PDS, for instance, there cannot be any chance of illegally diverting grains to the open market; procurement and storage costs are also higher in the PDS.

On the other hand, private retailers may demand excessive profit margins in order to enter the remote areas. So, the superiority of one system versus another is an empirical issue. This suggests that the sensible option is to allow both the systems to co-exist so as to enable the costs associated with the system get evaluated.

Notes

1. Madhura Swaminathan, "Excluding the Needy: The Public Provisioning of Food in India", *Social Scientist* 30 (3–4): March–April 2002.
2. C.B. Mamoria and Badri Bishal Tripathi, *Agricultural Problems of India*. Allahabad: Kitab Mahal, 2003, p. 844.
3. S.S. Chauhan, *The Food Problem*, 1958, pp. 1–2. Quoted in C.B. Mamoria and B.B. Tripathi, op. cit.
4. Report of the Famine Commission, Pt. I, 1880, p. 66.
5. Census of India Report, Pt. I-A, p. 164, 1951, p. 164.
6. C.B. Mamoria and Badri Bishal Tripathi, op. cit., p. 847.
7. Ibid.
8. Economic Survey 2007–08, Government of India, Ministry of Finance, p. 179.
9. Approximately 100 g of processed cereals and sugar-based foods can provide up to 200 kcals or more.
10. Reported in *The Economic Times*, 17 July 2009.

References

Amar Ujala, 4 March 2008.

Bhalla, G.S. "Demand and Supply of Food and Feed Grains by 2020", in *Towards Hunger Free India*, eds. M.D. Asthana and P. Medrano, New Delhi: Manohar, 2001.

Bhushan, R. and H. Damodaran. "Will Amul's Pizzas Trigger a Price War?", *Hindu Business Line*, 3 August 2001.

Census of India Report, Pt. I-A, 164, 1951.

Chand, R. "Wheat Exports: Little Gain", *Economic and Political Weekly*, 36 (25): 23 June 2001.

Chauhan, S.S. *The Food Problem*, 1958. Quoted in C.B. Mamoria and B.B. Tripathi, *Agricultural Problems of India*. Allahabad: Kitab Mahal, 2003.

Consumer Expenditure, Distribution and Poverty: Implications of NSSO 55th Round, Abhijit Sen (www.macroscan.org/onl/jan01/Abhijit-S en.pdf).

Damodaran, H. "Food Grains off Take Surges by 55 percent", *Business Line*, 21 January 2002.

Economic Survey, Government of India, Ministry of Finance, 2007–08.

Food Processing in India, Ministry of Food Processing Industries, Annual Report of Government of India, 2003 (www.cci.in/pdf/surveys_reports/food-processing-indiapdf).

George, P.S. Public Distribution of Food Grains in Kerala: Income Distribution, Implications and Effectiveness, IFPRI, Research Report, 7 March 1979.

Government of India, Focus on the Poor, Ministry of Civil Supplies, Consumer Affairs and Public Distribution, New Delhi, 1997.

Government of India, Ministry of Rural Areas and Employment, Department of Rural Employment and Poverty Alleviation, Letter No. M-28012/16/91-IRD.III, New Delhi, April 1997.

Kriesel, S. and S. Zaidi. The Targeted Public Distribution System in Uttar Pradesh, India: An Evaluation, Draft Paper, Washington: The World Bank, August 1997.

Krishnakumar. "Public Distribution System: A System in Peril", *Frontline* 17 (19), September 2000: 16–29.

Madura, S. "Excluding the Needy: The Public Provisioning of Food in India", *Social Scientist* 30 (3–4): March–April 2002.

Mamoria, C.B. and Badri Bishal Tripathi. *Agricultural Problems of India*. Allahabad: Kitab Mahal, 2003.

National Sample Survey Organisation, Ministry of Statistics and Programme Implementation, Government of India, 2001a, Consumption of Some Important Commodities in India, NSSO 55th Round Report No. 457, New Delhi, 1999–2000.

Pizzamarketplace.com, Pizza Continues Slicing into India Restaurant Market, News Story, 14 July 2003 (www.pizzamarketplace.com/news_story_16186htm).

Radhakrishnan, R. "Food and Nutrition Security", in *India Development Report*, eds. K. Parikh and R. Radhakrishanan, Delhi: Oxford University Press, 2002.

Rao, C.H. Hanumantha. "Declining Demand for Food Grains in Rural India: Causes and Implications", *Economic and Political Weekly* 35 (4): 2001.

Report of the Famine Commission, 1880.

Swarna Sadasivam Vepa, Impact of Globalization on Food Consumption of Urban India, paper prepared for the FAO technical workshop on "Globalization of Food Systems: Inputs on Food Security and Nutrition", Rome, 2003.

3

Poverty and Globalization

Indu Upadhyay

Social welfare aimed at development or improvement in well-being of the people is an important objective of the development planning. No doubt, economic growth is extremely important; it has to be accompanied by improvement in the quality of life of people for the development process to be sustainable in the long run. The motion of inclusive growth relates essentially to equality of opportunity to all for productive and meaningful life with freedom and dignity. In terms of policy measures, it requires emphasis on social sector development and programmes. The development of human resources contributes to sustained growth and productive employment. A healthy, educated and skilled workforce can more significantly and effectively contribute to economic development. The present chapter tries to study the problem of poverty even after the adoption of new economic reforms. The indicators selected for the purpose are human development, equality, hunger and unemployment.

Human Development and Gender Situation

The United Nations Development Programme (UNDP) has started presenting the Human Development Index (HDI) very recently in its annual Human Development Report. The HDI is simply an effort to measure the progress of human development in the developed and underdeveloped countries, which began with its publication in 1990. It is a composite index of four social indicators: life expectancy, adult literacy, years of schooling and real GDP per capita.

As per the UNDP's Global Human Development Report (HDR) 2007, in spite of the absolute value of HDI for India improving from 0.5777 in 2000 to 0.611 in 2005, the relative ranking of India has not changed much.[1] India ranks 128 among the countries with medium human development out of 177 countries of the world as against 126 in the year 2000. In terms of Gender Development Index (GDI), India ranks 113 out of 157 countries. Further, a zero count for HDI rank minus GDI rank is indicative of almost similar status of ranking in gender development and human development. At the same time, while India's HDI rank reflects low relative achievement in the level of human development, a negative count of (–11) for GDP per capita (PPP US $) rank minus HDI rank is also an indicative that the country has done better in terms of per capita income than in other components of human development. In other words, in spite of the increasing per capita income, the expenditure on education, nutritious food and medical facilities was not to the extent as it should be. The situation reinforces the need for greater focus on this area in our development planning. There are 60 doctors per one lakh people in India, which is 313 in Norway, which can be a cause of lower life expectancy at birth and higher maternal mortality ratio. The life expectancy at birth in India is 63.7 years which is 79.8 years in Norway. On the other hand, the percentage of infants with lower birth weight was 5 per cent in Norway, while it was 30 per cent in India. The statistics shown in Table 3.1 shows that India is in the grip of relative poverty, though it was expected that India will come in the line of developed nations after adoption of the policy of globalization. The reforms have resulted into freezing of

Table 3.1

India's Global Position on Human and Gender Development

Country	HDI Rank		GDP per Capita (ppp US $) Minus HDI Rank	GDI Rank		HDI Rank Minus GDI Rank	Life Expectancy of Birth (in years)	Combined GER (Primary, Secondary, Tertiary Education)	Physicians per One Lakh People	Infant with Low Birth Weight (in %)
	2000	2005		2000	2005					
Norway	1	2	1	3	3	–1	79.8	99.2	313	5
Australia	5	3	13	1	2	1	80.9	113	247	7
Sri Lanka	89	99	07	70	89	–1	71.6	62.7	55	22
China	96	81	05	77	73	1	72.5	69.1	106	4
Indonesia	110	107	06	91	94	1	69.7	68.2	13	9
India	124	128	–11	105	113	0	63.7	63.8	60	30
Pakistan	138	136	–8	120	125	–7	64.6	40	74	19
Bangladesh	145	140	0	121	121	1	63.1	56	26	36
Nepal	142	142	08	119	128	–4	62.6	58.1	21	21
Mozambique	170	172	–16	144	150	2	42.8	52.9	3	15
Niger	172	174	–1	146	155	–1	55.8	22.7	2	13

Source: UNDP Human Development Reports 2002 and 2007.

grants to many institutions and in stagnating if not lowering the expenditure[2] on sectors, namely, education and health to improve the living standard of the people. Social sector has made the condition of people more vulnerable. Now, it is the responsibility of the government to increase public expenditure on the needy.

Table 3.2 shows the trends in social sector expenditure. The central government expenditure on social services and rural development has gone up consistently over the years. The share of central government expenditure on social services including rural development in total expenditure (plan and non-plan) has increased from 10.46 per cent in 2003–04 to 19.4 per cent in 2009–10 (BE).[3]

Expenditure on social services, which include expenditure on sports, culture, medical and public health, family welfare, water supply and sanitation, housing, urban development, welfare of SCs, STs and OBCs, labour welfare, social security, nutrition, etc. There is an increasing trend of expenditure on social services by the general government in recent years. The social expenditure by the government was ₹ 1,72,812 crore in 2004–05, which increased to 18,70,955 crore in 2009–10. It reflects the high priority attached to these sectors. The expenditure on social sector as a proportion of total expenditure was 19.9 per cent in 2004–05 which increased to 24 per cent in 2008–09, but in the year 2009–10 it has declined to 23.8 per cent. Expenditure on education as a percentage of social service expenditure declined from 48.7 per cent in 2004–05 to 44.6 per cent in 2009–10. In case of health also, it declined from 21.7 per cent in 2004–05 to 20 per cent in 2009–10. It seems that the declining expenditure of health and education has lowered human development and gender development ranks for India.

It should however be pointed out that the fresh hunger map of the world and the India State Hunger Index (ISHI) published by International Food Policy Research Institute have made lots of revelations about louder slogans on socio-economic development of the country, foreign direct investment in all sectors to improve the quality of life and vigorous industrialization at the cost of poor

Table 3.2

Trends in Social Services Expenditure by Central Government (Central and State Governments Combined)

(in ₹ Crores)

Item	*2004–05 (Actual)*	*2005–06 (Actual)*	*2006–07 (Actual)*	*2007–08 (Actual)*	*2008–09 (Actual)*	*2009–10 (BE)*
Total Expenditure	8,69,757	9,50,855	11,09,174	12,95,003	16,59,100	18,70,955
Expenditure on Social Services	1,72,812	2,02,872	2,30,340	2,88,500	3,08,280	4,45,751
(1) Education	84,111	96,385	1,14,744	1,27,547	1,67,081	1,08,842
(2) Health	37,535	45,428	52,128	60,839	78,489	89,314
(3) Others	51,168	60,879	72,470	1,00,084	1,54,358	1,57,595
As a Percentage of GDP						
Total Expenditure	26.85	25.90	25.89	26.19	29.78	30.35
Expenditure on Social Services	5.33	5.47	5.59	5.83	7.15	7.23
(1) Education	2.60	2.60	2.68	2.58	3.01	3.26
(2) Health	1.16	1.23	1.22	1.23	1.37	1.45
(3) Others	1.58	1.64	1.69	2.02	2.77	2.56

Cont'd...

...Cont'd

As a Percentage of Total Expenditure						
Expenditure on Social Services	19.9	21.1	21.6	22.3	24.0	23.8
(1) Education	9.7	10.0	10.3	9.9	10.1	10.6
(2) Health	4.3	9.7	4.7	4.7	4.5	4.8
(3) Others	5.9	6.3	6.5	7.7	9.3	8.4
As a Percentage of Social Service Expenditure						
(1) Education	48.7	47.5	47.9	44.2	42.1	44.6
(2) Health	21.7	22.4	21.8	21.1	19.2	20.0
(3) Others	29.6	30.0	30.3	34.7	38.7	35.4

BE: Budget Estimates; RE: Revised Estimates.

Source: RBI is obtained from Budget Documents of Union and State Governments.

people's livelihood. According to report, India's Global Hunger India (GHI) score is 23.7 which gives it the rank 65 out of 84 countries. The index ranks countries on a 100-point scale, with 0 being the best score (no hunger) and 100 being the worst. Countries who have been ranked as better performers with less percentage on hunger are Nigeria, Kenya, Cambodia, Rwanda, Pakistan, etc. (Alarming Poverty in India: Global Hunger Index 2009, 17 October 2009, Cyber Gandhi; escape from india.word.press.com/2009/alarming-poverty-in-india-global-hungerindex-2009).

It needs no emphasis that poverty in India can be defined as a situation when a certain section of people are unable to fulfil their basic needs. Since 1972, poverty has been defined on the basis of money required to buy food worth 2,100 calories in urban areas and 2,400 calories in rural areas. The incidence of poverty is estimated by the Planning Commission on the basis of quinquennial large sample surveys on household consumer expenditure conducted by National Sample Survey Organization (NSSO). The Uniform Recall Period (URP) consumption distribution data of NSS 61st round yields a poverty ratio of 28.3 per cent in rural areas, 25.7 per cent in urban areas and 27.5 per cent for the country as a whole in 2004–05. The corresponding poverty ratios from Mixed Recall Period (MRP) consumption data are 21.8 per cent for rural areas, 21.7 per cent for urban areas and 21.8 per cent for the country as a whole. While the former uses consumption data for 30-day recall/reference period for all items of consumption, the latter uses 365-day recall/reference period for five frequently purchased non-food items, namely, clothing, footwear, durable goods, education and medical expenses, and a 30-day recall/reference period for the remaining items. According to Table 3.3, the percentage of poor in 2004–05 estimated from URP consumption, distribution of NSS was 36 per cent for the country as a whole, which declined to 27.5 per cent in 2004–05. The percentage of poor in 2004–05 estimated from MRP consumption distribution was 21.8 per cent which declined from 26.1 per cent in 1999–2000.

Table 3.3

Poverty Ratios by URP and MRP (in %)

Category	*1993–94*	*2004–05*
By Uniform Recall Period (URP) Method		
Rural	37.3	28.3
Urban	32.4	25.7
All India	36.0	27.5
	1999–2000	*2004–05*
By Mixed Recall Period (MRP) Method		
Rural	27.1	21.8
Urban	23.6	21.7
All India	26.1	21.8

Source: Economic Survey 2007–08, Government of India, Ministry of Finance, p. 243.

The average per capita consumption expenditure for rural and urban populations as per the 61st round 2004–05 is ₹ 558.78 and ₹ 1,052.36, respectively. The NSSO data also reveal that the rural population on an average spends 55 per cent on consumption of food and the remaining 45 per cent on non-food items (Table 3.4).

Table 3.4

Consumption Patterns Across Different MPCE Classes of Population (Rural) (in %)

	Food	*Non-Food*
Poor (roughly below PL)		
0–235	68.45	31.55
235–270	67.16	32.84

Cont'd...

...Cont'd

270–320	66.35	33.65
320–365[a]	64.78	35.20
Roughly between PL and 2 PL		
365–410	63.99	36.01
410–455	62.93	37.06
455–510	61.61	38.39
510–580[b]	60.11	39.88
580–690	58.02	41.98
690–890	53.92	46.08
Roughly above 2 PL		
890–1155	49.80	50.20

[a] MPCE class having poverty line (PL) at ₹ 365.30.

[b] MPCE class having 1.5 times the poverty line (1.5 PL) at ₹ 534.45.

[c] MPCE class having twice the poverty line (2PL) at ₹ 712.60.

Source: NSSO; Estimated from Table 5R of NSS Report No. 508: Level and Pattern of Consumer Expenditure 2004–05.

It needs no emphasis that rural poor below the PL are spending 31 to 35 per cent of their total income on non-food items and remaining on food items. In the group of population between PL and 2PL, non-food items take up 36 per cent and 46 per cent, respectively of the total consumption expenditure. A similar classification of urban population is shown in Table 3.5.

About 42.51 per cent of the total consumption on an average is spent on food items and the remaining 57.48 per cent on non-food items. However, in the group of population between PL and 2PL, non-food items take up between 45 and 53 per cent of the total consumption expenditure which was 36 and 46 per cent for the rural population. The point to be noticed is that the average consumption pattern of urban and rural populations in general is more skewed in favour of non-food items.

Table 3.5

Consumption Patterns Across Different MPCE Classes of Population (Urban) (in %)

	Food	*Non-Food*
Poor (roughly below PL)		
0–335	64.86	35.14
335–395	63.11	36.89
395–485	60.04	39.96
485–580[a]	57.30	42.70
Roughly between PL and 2PL		
580–675	55.35	44.65
675–790	52.37	47.62
790–930[b]	46.69	50.31
930–1100[c]	46.61	53.39
Roughly above 2PL		
1100–1380	44.44	55.56
1380–1880	40.17	59.83

[a] MPCE class having poverty line (PL) at ₹ 583.60.

[b] MPCE class having poverty line (PL) (1.5 PL) at ₹ 807.90.

[c] MPCE class having twice the poverty line (2PL) at ₹ 1,077.20.

Source: NSSO: Estimated from Table SU of NSS Report No. 508: Level and Pattern of Consumer Expenditure 2004–05.

It should however be pointed out that a committee constituted by the Ministry of Rural Development for suggesting a methodology for estimation of BPL households in rural areas observed that the national poverty line at ₹ 356 per capita per month in rural areas and in urban areas at ₹ 539 per capita per month in 2004–05, permitted both rural and urban people to consume about 1,820 kcal as against the desired norm of 2,400/2,100 kcal. Hence, a large number of the rural poor get left out of the BPL status benefits as in order to consume the desired norm of 2,400/2,100 kcal; the cut-off line for determining BPL status should be ₹ 700 in rural areas and ₹ 1,000 in urban areas. The committee therefore recommended that the people titled to BPL status should be revised upwards at least to 50 per cent though the above norm of 2,400 kcal would require this to be 80 per cent. The committee further observed that at any given time, the calorie intake of the poorest quartile continues to be 30–50 per cent less than the calorie intake of the top quartile of the population, despite it needing more calories because of harder manual work. Not only has this calorie consumption of the bottom 50 per cent of the population been consistently decreasing since 1987, which is a matter of concern. Thus, the recommendation of the committee suggests an increase in BPL families' coverage. This in turn implies automatic expansion in the coverage of BPL families, which in turn implies expansion in the coverage of the public distribution system (PDS) and other government schemes where beneficiaries are decided on BPL basis. For this purpose, additional public expenditure is also required.

As is clear from the previous table that poverty is on an increase in spite of the adoption of New Economic Policy in India. It is necessary to look into the position of the poor regarding the availability of some of the basic necessities for better living. It needs no emphasis that under the constitutional diversion of responsibility between the centre and state governments, the bulk of social services and most infrastructure services lie in the domain of state governments. Thus, both the level of social sector expenditure at state level and its quality effectiveness have a direct bearing on the human development outcomes and the overall well-being. While there has been some increase in the social sector spending at state level, the central government has also stepped up its outlay on social sectors and rural development programmes substantially in recent year through centrally-sponsored schemes. There is much that still needs to be done in terms of improving social sector and human development outcomes at the state level. Table 3.6 illustrates various facts regarding some of the indicators of poverty in states of India. The table clearly indicates that the percentage of population below the poverty line is highest in

Table 3.6

Socio-economic Profile of Major States

Items	*A.P.*	*Assam*	*Bihar*	*Gujarat*	*Haryana*	*H.P.*	*Karnataka*	*Kerala*	*M.P.*
[1] Poverty and Growth Related % of Population BPL (2004–05)	15.8	19.7	41.4	16.8	14	10	25	15	38.3
Average MPCE (2004–05)									
[2] Rural	586	543	417	596	863	798	508	1,013	439.06
[3] Urban	1,019	1,058	696	1,115	1,142	1,390	1,033	1,291	903.68
[4] Inadequate Food (2004–05) (% Households)	0.5	5	2.7	0.2	0.1	0	0	2.3	1.6
Lorenz Ratio (2004–05)									
[5] Rural	0.288	0.197	0.208	0.268	0.323	0.295	0.264	0.341	0.269
[6] Urban	0.37	0.314	0.339	0.304	0.361	0.318	0.365	0.4	0.397
Health Related									
[7] Life Expectancy at Birth (2001–05)	64.1	58.7	61.4	63.9	65.9	66.8	65.1	73.9	57.7
[8] Infant Mortality Rates (2006)	56	67	60	53	57	50	48	15	74
[9] Births Assisted by a Doctor/Nurse/LHV/ANM/Other Health Personnel (%)	74.2	31.2	30.9	64.7	54.2	50.2	71.3	99.7	37.1

Cont'd...

...Cont'd

[10] Institutional Births (%)	68.6	22.7	22	54.6	39.4	45.3	66.9	99.5	29.7
Facilities at PHCs (%) (as in March 2005)									
[11] With Labour Room	100	NA	13	67	71	NA	100	14	19
[12] With Operation Theatre	87	NA	13	67	71	36	NA	12	63
[13] With 24 Hours Delivery Facility	30	NA	14	5	51	NA	24	7	NA
Education Related									
[14] GER (6–14 years) (2004–05) Total	87.0	92.0	65.2	101.7	80.0	108.7	98.8	95.4	95.4
[15] GER (14–16 years) (2004–05) Total	53.1	49.4	22.5	55.3	53.0	134.9	59.0	93.2	93.2
[16] GER (16–18 years) (2004–05) Total	42.2	14.4	9.8	21.8	34.2	127.7	33.9	27.9	27.9
Basic Amenities Related									
[17] % of Households Having Electricity (2005–06)	88.4	38.1	27.7	89.3	91.5	98.4	89.3	91	91
[18] % of Households Having Access to Toilet Facility (2005–06)	42.4	76.4	25.2	54.6	52.3	45.6	46.5	96	96
[19] % of Households Having Safe Drinking Water Facilities (2001)	80.1	58.8	86.6	84.1	86.1	88.6	84.6	23.4	23.4

Cont'd...

Table 3.6: Columns continued...

Items	Maharashtra	Orissa	Punjab	Rajasthan	Tamil Nadu	U.P.	W.B.	Chhattisgarh	Jharkhand	All India
[1]	30.7	46.4	8.4	22.1	22.5	32.8	24.7	20.9	40.3	27.5
[2]	567.76	398.89	846.75	590.83	602.17	532.63	562.11	425.1	425.3	559
[3]	1148.27	757.31	1326.09	964.02	1079.65	857.05	1123.61	989.97	985.43	1052
[4]	0.8	5.3	0.7	0	0.3	1.5	9	2.2	0.6	1.9
[5]	0.31	0.302	0.278	0.248	0.315	0.287	0.273	0.305	0.231	0.297
[6]	0.371	0.355	0.393	0.367	0.358	0.37	0.376	0.439	0.354	0.373
[7]	66.9	59.2	69.2	61.7	66	59.8	64.6			63.2
[8]	35	73	44	67	37	71	38	61	49	57
[9]	70.7	46.4	68.6	43.2	93.2	29.2	45.7	44.3	28.7	48.2
[10]	66.1	38.7	52.5	32.2	90.4	22	43.1	15.7	19.2	40.7
[11]	68	64	39	83	100	0	44	20	NA	—
[12]	74	33	33	83	27	0	0	10	NA	—
[13]	99	9	17	NA	19	NA	11	100	NA	—
[14]	105.7	108.5	72.6	102.7	114.0	87.0	94.7	112.6	75.8	93.5
[15]	68.9	53.7	51.5	43.9	80.7	48.9	41.5	43.9	26.5	51.7
[16]	42.3	32.9	27.9	21.6	43.9	22.9	21.1	30.4	2.5	27.8
[17]	83.5	45.4	96.3	66.1	88.6	42.8	52.5	71.4	40.2	67.9
[18]	53	19.3	70.8	30.8	42.9	33.1	59.5	18.7	22.6	44.5
[19]	79.8	64.2	97.6	68.2	85.6	87.8	88.5	70.5	42.6	77.9

Note: UP includes Jharkhand – NFHS-3, O/o RGI.

Source: Based on the data obtained from Planning Commission, NSSO, NHP-2006, HS-2006 and Ministry of HRD.

Orissa, followed by Bihar, Chhattisgarh, Jharkhand and Madhya Pradesh, Punjab followed by Himachal Pradesh, Haryana, Kerala and Andhra Pradesh have low poverty. Prevalence of hunger is measured in months in which any member of the household had inadequate food which is unusually high in West Bengal. It is nine months for West Bengal, followed by Orissa having 5.3, Assam (5), Bihar (2.7), but it is lower in Himachal Pradesh (0), Rajasthan (0), Haryana (0.1), Gujarat (0.2), Karnataka (0.2) and Tamil Nadu (0.3). Further, inequality in consumption, as measured by Lorenz Ratio, is highest in Chhattisgarh followed by Kerala, Madhya Pradesh, Punjab and West Bengal in urban areas. The inequality is low in urban Gujarat followed by Assam and Himachal Pradesh. Inequality in rural India is lower than in urban India in all the major states. In rural India, inequality is highest in Kerala, followed by Haryana, Tamil Nadu and Maharashtra. Assam has the lowest inequality, followed by Bihar, Jharkhand and Rajasthan in rural areas. Regarding health-related indicators, life expectancy is highest in Kerala (73.9), followed by Punjab (69.2), Maharashtra (66.9), Himachal Pradesh (66.8) and Tamil Nadu (66). It was least in Madhya Pradesh. As in March 2006, 100 per cent Primary Health Centres (PHCs) had a labour room in Andhra Pradesh, while it was low in Uttar Pradesh (0%), Bihar (13%), Kerala (14%) and Madhya Pradesh (19%). In March 2006, the proportion of PHCs with operation theatres was 87 per cent in Andhra Pradesh followed by Rajasthan (83%), Maharashtra (74%), Haryana (71%) and Gujarat (67%). It was low in Uttar Pradesh at (0), West Bengal (0), Chhattisgarh (10%), Kerala (12%) and Bihar (13%).

Education is any act or experience that has a formative effect on the mind, character or physical ability of an individual. In its technical sense, education is the process by which the society deliberately transmits its accumulated knowledge, skills and values from one generation to another. In 2004–05, the Gross Enrolment Ratios (GER) for elementary education, i.e., I to VIII (6–14 years) was highest in Madhya Pradesh (114.1%), followed by Tamil Nadu (114%) and Chhattisgarh (112.6%). It was lowest in Bihar (65.2%) followed by Punjab (72.6%) and Jharkhand (75.8%). In case of secondary education (IX–X classes), it was high in Himachal Pradesh (134.9%) followed by Kerala (93%) and Tamil Nadu (80.7%). It was lowest in Bihar (22.5%), Jharkhand (26.5%) and West Bengal (41.5%). For senior secondary level (XI–XII classes), GER was least at 2.5 per cent in Jharkhand followed by 9.8 per cent in Bihar and highest at 127.7 per cent for Himachal Pradesh followed by 43.9 per cent in Tamil Nadu.

In relation of basic necessities, Himachal Pradesh, Punjab, Haryana, Kerala, Karnataka, Gujarat, Tamil Nadu and Andhra Pradesh have much larger percentage of households having electricity than is the case in Bihar, Assam, Jharkhand, Uttar Pradesh and Orissa. Households having access to toilet facilities are high in Kerala, Assam and Punjab and low in Chhattisgarh, Jharkhand, Bihar and Madhya Pradesh.

Unemployment

It should however be pointed out that one of the indicators of poverty is unemployment that occurs when a person is available and willing to work but is currently without work. The point to be noted is that economic reforms may have given a boost to industrial productivity and brought in foreign investment in capital intensive areas. But the boom has not created jobs. This was not expected. According to a report by Washington-based Institute of Policy Studies (IPS), the combined sales of the world's top MNCs is now greater than the combined GDP of all but the world's nine largest national economies. Yet, the total direct employment generated by these multinationals is merely 18.8 millions – one hundredth of one per cent of the global workforce (www.indiaonestop.com/unemployment.htm).

Table 3.7 indicates that employment growth during 1999–2000 to 2004–05 has accelerated significantly as compared to the growth witnessed during 1999–2000 to 2004–05, about 47 million work opportunities were created compared to only 24 million in the period 1993–94 to 1999–2000. Employment growth accelerated from 1.25 per cent to 2.84 per cent per annum. However, since the labour force grew at a faster rate of 2.84 per cent than the workforce, unemployment also rose.[4]

Table 3.7

Employment and Unemployment in Million Persons/Year (by CDS basis)

	1983 (in million)	*1993–94 (in million)*	*1999–2000 (in million)*	*2004–05 (in million)*	*Growth p.a. (in %)*		
					1983 to 1993–94	*1993–94 to 1999–2000*	*1999–2000 to 2004–05*
Population	718.10	893.68	1005.05	1092.83	2.11	1.98	1.80
Labour Force	263.82	334.20	364.88	419.65	2.28	1.47	2.84
Workforce	239.49	313.93	338.19	384.91	2.61	1.25	2.62
Unemployment Rate (%)	9.22	606	7.31	8.28	—	—	—
No. of Unemployed	24.34	20.27	26.68	34.74	—	—	—

Source: Various rounds of NSSO Survey on Employment and Unemployment/Planning Commission.

The employment growth in the organized sector shows somewhat different trend. Employment growth has declined during 1994–2007 in public and private sectors taken together. This has primarily happened due to the decline of employment in the public organized sector. Employment in establishments covered by the Employment Market Information System of the Ministry of Labour grew at 1.20 per cent per annum during 1983–94, but decelerated to –0.03 per cent per annum during 1994–2007. However, the latter decline was mainly due to a decrease in employment in the public sector establishments from 1.53 per cent in the earlier period to –0.57 per cent in the later period, whereas the private sector showed acceleration in the pace of growth of employment from 0.44 per cent to 1.30 per cent per annum (Table 3.8).

Employment opportunities in the current financial year were affected by the global financial crisis and economic slowdown in India. It should however be pointed out that while comprehensive employment data for the current financial year are not available, some sample surveys conducted by the Labour Bureau, Ministry of Labour and Employment indicated employment losses in the wake of financial crisis and economic slowdown. According to the Economic Survey, the government was concerned about the possible impact of the financial crisis on the Indian economy, including employment and several measures, financial and fiscal were taken[5] to deal with the problem. Despite the success of some recent measures taken by the government to alleviate the impact of the economic crisis, employment level continued to decline.

Table 3.8

Rate of Growth of Employment in Organized Sector (percentage per annum)

	1983–94	*1994–2007*
Public Sector	1.53	–0.57
Private Sector	0.44	1.30
Total Organized	1.20	–0.03

Source: Eleventh Five-Year Plan Document and Ministry of Labour and Employment.

Inequality

One of the indicators of relative poverty is inequality. The rate of increasing disparity between the "haves" and "have-nots" is increasing day by day. Inequality in India in comparison to other countries as reflected in the Gini Index which is a measure of unequal distribution of income or consumption among individuals or households is given in the HDR 2009. The lower (higher) the number, more equal is the distribution. India's Gini Index was at 36.8 and was more favourable than that of comparable countries such as Brazil (55), Turkey (43.2), Thailand (42.5), China (41.5), Indonesia (39.4), Vietnam (37.8) and even USA (40.8), Singapore (42.5), Hong Kong (43.4) and Portugal (38.5). When the richest 10 per cent of the population was compared to the poorest 10 per cent of the population in India, the Gini Index stood at 8.6 which was also lower than the countries compared above, they had otherwise ranked very high in human development.[6]

Inter-state inequality in India as reflected in the Lorenz ratio (which like Gini Index is used as measure of relative inequality) has been estimated by the NSSO based household consumer expenditure for 2004–05 (as shown in Table 3.7). For rural India, the Lorenz ratio for total consumption expenditure was 0.30, while for urban India it was 0.37, indicating a higher inequality in urban areas. Lower inequality was seen in the rural areas of Assam (0.197), Meghalaya (0.155) and Manipur (0.158) than in Kerala (0.341), Haryana (0.323), Tamil Nadu (0.315) and Maharashtra (0.310). Similarly, lower inequality was seen in the urban areas of Arunachal Pradesh (0.243), Jammu and Kashmir (0.244), Meghalaya (0.258) and Manipur (0.175) than in Chhattisgarh (0.439), Goa (0.405), Kerala (0.400) and Madhya Pradesh (0.397). Disparity in consumption of durable goods was much higher than in consumption of cereals.[7]

India with a billion-plus population has a booming economy, significant part of the population features in the world's richest list. But still poverty remains the biggest menace today. It should however be pointed out that the neo-liberal approaches to poverty alleviation, as prescribed by the structural adjustment initiatives that modify macroeconomic policies in impoverished nations, are intended to spur growth. Yet, a fundamental observation exists that the neo-liberal prescription has functioned to increase poverty. Proponents of this view argue that policy and programmes based on neo-liberal ideology tend to include rhetoric supporting the movement of the poor towards self-sufficiency and independence, yet in reality by focusing on the poor as the root of the problem, these type of initiatives have served to increase dependency rather than creating the gains they promised (Kilty and Segal, 2004). The International Monetary Fund (IMF) and World Bank have prescribed structural adjustment policies that notably cut back in health, education and other vital social services around the world as a condition for loan and repayment. In conjunction with these cut backs, the sector adjustment policies in support of globalization and free trade open up the economies, resources, labour, markets and competition among the developing countries as well as with more powerful and established industrialized nations.

Conclusion

On one hand, the ideology of globalization and neo-liberalism, through structural adjustment lending, at its best opens up international trade markets for export-led growth opportunities to the developing countries. Conversely, the same ideology in some cases has led to increased poverty and resulted into a situation where "to attract investment, poor countries enter a spiralling race to the bottom to see who can provide lower standards, reduced wages and cheaper resources. This has increased poverty and inequality for most people. It also forms a backbone what we today call globalization. As a result, it maintains the historic unequal rule trade" (Shah, 2007).

An ideology shift in the rhetoric of structural adjustment programmes to emphasize poverty eradication and human development through the poverty reduction and growth facility (PRGF) occurred in 1999, yet neo-liberation and globalization have fallen short on commitments to combat poverty. Ideally, macro-economic growth was to occur with a critical eye on the poverty line, yet by eliminating the trade barriers of poorer countries (in the form of regulating their exports and encouraging imports), while maintaining their own wealth, western countries have functioned to produce increasing levels of economic disparity and vulnerability in the developing countries across globe (Siglitz, 2003: 6).

While it could be argued that other factors also have conditions of developing countries, it must be acknowledged that in spite of the structural adjustment policies and the commitment of the powers that support them, poverty has persisted in urban and rural communities worldwide. Despite the intentions of the prevailing neo-liberal consciousness, poverty continues to manifest globally as hunger and malnutrition; illness and related morbidity and mortality, limited or lack of access to basic education, sanitation and social services; homelessness and inadequate housing; crime; social isolation; and economic, political, social and cultural marginalization (United Nations, 1995). The mass of well-intentioned investments in public policies and intervention across the globe has yet to yield a definitive response to the problem of how to alleviate poverty.

The adoption of strategy that bridges the gap between economic and human development approaches to poverty alleviation is suggested as an alternative to the standard neo-liberal approach. This strategy would go beyond calculating needs and progress based upon economic indicators to include a focus on the non-income based capacity of individuals, communities, countries or regions to eradicate poverty. This comprehensive economic and human development strategy to poverty alleviation would enable public authorities to adeptly progress towards macroeconomic development while meeting the demand for public accountability. It is recommended that a strategy would also require increased flexibility to address non-economic based issues in local context.

Amartya Sen and Martha Nussbaum started an international trend towards assessing non-economic based assets and capabilities to alleviate poverty (Grusky and Kanbur, 2002). Their strategy involved capturing such indicators as access to technology, water, sanitation, education, employment and healthcare; social, political and economic inclusion and human capital development. These non-monetary indicators of poverty allow for the complexities of the contextual nature of poverty to be assessed. The reduced reliance on economic measures of progress and increased use of non-economic measures is suggested.

The ongoing assessment should emphasize measures of inclusion. In addition to improving access to technology, the ability of individuals to effectively exercise their voices in social, economic and political affairs can contribute to the collective capacity of groups, communities and nations to meet their basic needs. Together with traditional economic-based measures, the indicators listed above can provide organizations interested in supporting economic growth in developing countries with comprehensive view of the types of interventions or strategies needed to also move individuals out of poverty.

In addition to modifying the measures of progress, strategies and interventions developed to boost the economy and eradicate poverty should be grounded and sustainable social policy should be framed. Innovative reform should include the possibilities for asset redistribution through low-income cooperative housing and enterprise development initiatives, and provide the means for men and women to access credit and build their capacity for wealth attainment (Heintz and Jardine, 1998). Not only this, traditional social reforms should be coupled with macroeconomic polity that seeks to achieve the creation of and access to liveable wage-paying employment and training designed to meet needs in high demand markets and improve access to services that meet basic needs such as education, sanitation, healthcare and housing. These reforms need not be solely government driven, but should include the collective participation of the private sector, media and civil society. Non-traditional social reforms and legislation should also be established that facilitate the transformation of gender ideologies and relationships in public and private spheres that reconceptualize gender roles with the household and workplace. To reverse the trend of persistent poverty for women, training and education particularly for occupation where women have been historically under-presented, childcare support, enforced anti-employment discrimination and anti-domestic violence legislation and programmes that enhance women's credit, and home and business ownership opportunities are needed. The possibility exists that to effectively address the neo-liberal ideals of economic growth and poverty reduction for the developing nations, their demonstrable commitment to work in partnership with international interests to develop policies and programmes that target women's labour force participation, particularly in educational and occupational areas where women have been under-presented is required.

This analysis centres upon the neo-liberal approach to poverty eradication in the Indian context, the implications derived from the assessment transcend national and regional boundaries. An anecdotal perspective that views neo-liberalism in the Indian context as a local anomaly would miss the opportunity to observe and understand the ways in which local events may come to have global consequences. A primary recommendation emerging from the chapter is that for assessing poverty eradication in the era of globalization and neo-liberalism should be, such that it can at once magnify the impact of distant events on local experience as well as the global consequences of local developments (Held, McGrew, Goldblatt and Perraton, 1999). It is suggested to use an integrated analytical framework that advances an understanding of the universal and particular as a means to articulate and facilitate the flow of social and economic capital within and between local, regional and global contexts.

The government's strategy of inclusive growth in recent years is reflected in programmes such as Bharat Nirman aimed at improving the quality of life of people living in rural areas. Besides, schemes such as the Mahatma Gandhi National Rural Employment Guarantee Scheme (MNREGS) have ensured that the rural poor are left with sufficient purchasing power for their basic requirements, especially food, through guaranteed employment. The recent revamp of the SJSRY reflects the government's commitment towards alleviation of urban poverty also. However, the government needs to look into further convergence of schemes. There is also a need to reduce the overlap between schemes being implemented by different departments at the centre and in the states, as well as between those implemented by the centre and states.

In spite of increased government outlays in the social sector in recent years, lack of identity proof results in harassment and denial of services to the poor and marginalized. As a result, there are still leakages in the programmes/schemes and the benefits do not reach the intended target groups of individuals/people in full. Providing identity proof to the poor and the marginalized through the UIDAI (Unique Identification Authority of India) will enhance their access to government services, both at state and central levels, and will enable smoother delivery of direct benefits to the poor and underserved. Specifically, it will improve the delivery of the flagship schemes of the central government. This will also prevent leakages as well as wastages in the implementation of these schemes. Success in reaching this objective can be further assured through involvement of local communities and PRIs.

Notes

1. Economic Survey 2007–08, Government of India, Ministry of Finance, p. 239.
2. Anand Teltumbde, *Globalization and Dalits*. Nagpur: Sanket Prakashan, 2001, p. 36.
3. Economic Survey 2009–10, Government of India, Ministry of Finance, p. 272.
4. Economic Survey 2007–08, Government of India, Ministry of Finance, p. 247.
5. Economic Survey 2009–10, Government of India, Ministry of Finance, p. 276.
6. Ibid., p. 275.
7. Ibid.

References

Grusky, D.B. and R. Kanbur, eds. *Poverty and Inequalities*. California: Stanford University Press, 2002.

Heintz, J. and C. Jardine. "Poverty and Economics", Report to South African Poverty Hearings, Johannesburg, NALEDI, 1998.

Held, D., A. McGrew, D. Goldblatt and J. Perraton. *Global Transformation: Politics, Economics and Culture*. Cambridge: Polity; Stanford: University Press, 1999.

Kilty, K.M. and E.A. Segal. "Poverty and Inequality in Latin American – US Borderlands: Implications of US Interventions", *Journal of Poverty* 8 (4), 2004: 1–6.

Shah, A. Corruption: Global Issues, 2007 (http://www.globalissues.org/TradeRelated/Poverty/Corruption.asp).

Siglitz, J. *Globalization and its Discontents*. New York: W.W. Norton, 2003.

United Nations, Report of the World Summit for Social Development in Copenhagen, 1995.

4

Globalization and the Banaras Silk Industry

A Case Study of Weavers of Banaras

Ellina Samantroy and Indu Upadhyay

The closure of traditional looms all over Uttar Pradesh is a matter of serious concern for the government as it is creating a situation of joblessness for Banarasi silk sari weavers. The handloom industry at Varanasi (Banaras) which has received acclamation worldwide for its rich and intricately woven saris is facing severe crisis today jeopardizing all the avenues and opportunities of the poor weavers. Of the six lakh weavers in the state, over half have been forced to take up menial jobs such as pulling rickshaws in the cities of eastern Uttar Pradesh. In 2003, three weavers in Varanasi district committed suicide as they were unable to repay the loans they had taken to try and revive their trade. The industry is passing through a recession and although the Uttar Pradesh government recently levied a 12.5 per cent tax on power looms to help the handloom weavers, the move has not helped much. Over the last few years, the export of Banarasi silk has dwindled. A slump in the international market has hit the industry. Besides, China silk traders have moved cheap yarn into the local market and have decided to replicate Banarasi silk by hiring weavers from Varanasi. In this context, it is a matter of serious concern for policy-makers and social scientists to explore the socio-economic conditions of the weavers of Varanasi city and deeply probe into the matter so that a thorough understanding is established about the importance of the handloom industry. So, the present paper attempts to focus on the way production is organized and the social relations involved. An attempt is also made to explore the threats to the Banaras silk industry and the nature of crisis the silk weavers are undergoing.

Historical Background

One of the oldest living cities in the world, Varanasi for thousands of years has been a sacred place in northern India. For more than 1,000 years, this city has been home to the largest number of handloom weavers in India. Varanasi fabrics were once used to adorn the bodies of royalty and common people alike. These fabrics shine and stand out with their myriad colours, their intricate and bold designs, and their unique aesthetic quality. Varanasi weavers' inspiration and philosophy is expressed well in the quote of Kabir, the 15th century poet and weaver from Varanasi, who said "God Almighty is also a weaver ... he weaves unique designs for everyone"! The use of printing blocks is as old as 3000 BC and India used to export fabrics back to China in as early as 4th century BC Jacquard Loom invented in 1805 is still being used today. Varanasi silk is called "Taj Mahal of Indian Silk". Some people believe it has reference in Rig Veda (Hirayana Vastra). However, sari weaving reached its zenith in the Mughal era.

The history of the silk industry in India is traditionally linked to the Muslim community which for almost 800 years was in charge of the production. The manufacture trade of silk fabrics has constituted a significant part of the economy of Banaras since pre-mughal times. Once Muslims settled in the city, they became the weaver class and silk fabrics acquired motifs and designs of

Islamic provenance (Showeb, 1994). As a result of the mercantile nature of the city's economy and the trade generated by its status as an important centre of Hindu pilgrimage, the silk business flourished (see Pandey, 1981). In Varanasi, weaving has historically been the occupation of the low-status sections of the Sunni Muslim community, traditionally called "Julahas". While low-ranking Sunni Muslims have constituted the main workforce, the wholesale business in silk fabrics has historically belonged to the city's Hindu communities of traders, landlords and money-lenders, such as Gujaratis, Agarwals, Punjabis, Khattris, Marwaris and Sindhis (Kumar, 1988: 80), who have migrated to the city over the centuries. Over time, the main division of labour between Hindu and Muslim communities changed in terms of who controlled the domains of production and trade. In her well-known account of the artisans of Banaras, Nita Kumar has highlighted their communal solidarity, arguing that irrespective of the socio-economic backgrounds of different communities in Banaras, "the nature of Hindu-Muslim relations in the city is exceptional" (1989: 168). Until 1960, the weavers were mainly Muslim, while trade was in the hands of the Hindu Marwaris. Beginning in the 1960s, some of the textile workers began selling products themselves, taking over a larger and larger segment of the market. Competition between Muslims and Hindus in selling textile products led to tension between the two communities, joining other problems of an economic, social and religious nature. The division of labour along religious communities with weaving industry and the changes that this division underwent in the 20th century are intertwined with the history of communal relations in the region as well as its economic vicissitudes. In major centres of cloth production such as Lucknow and Banaras, the weavers and spinners faced violent fluctuations in the conditions of their trade in the immediate pre-colonial, as well as early colonial period. A sharp increase in the demand for their goods and skills in the later 18th and early 19th century was followed by a progressive erosion of the markets. One result in the long term was a forced shift from the manufacture of fine cloths to that of coarser and cheaper varieties; the silk industry of Banaras stands out as a notable exception in this respect, but even here new markets arose some time after the collapse of the old and the weavers were not able to easily protect themselves from fluctuations in demand (Pandey, 1990: 72).

The 19th century and the following period testify to these fluctuations in the Banaras silk industry. In the mid-1880s, the Banaras weaving industry registered a period of crisis. By the 1920s, however, it witnessed a turn around, part of the overall industrial growth in the towns of Allahabad, Banaras, Lucknow and Kanpur, as a result of the "processes of mercantile accumulation and changing investment pattern and business priorities of urban *sarrafs*, moneylenders or bankers, who also financed trade" (Gooptu, 2001: 34). A multitude of small-scale units manufacturing a range of goods arose in these towns and led to what Gooptu terms "bazaar industrialization" (ibid.: 35), which in sarrafs' investment was founded on the existence of intermediaries employing artisans on a putting-out basis (ibid.: 37). Since the 1930s, the sari became the main artefact within the silk-weaving industry over all other traditional fabrics in Banaras (Kumar, 1988: 2). The early 1930s also coincided with the period of agrarian depression and the subsequent years were marked by strong industrial growth that continued the spurt begun in 1920s, most likely as a result of the concentration of capital in urban trade rather than agriculture (Gooptu, 2001: 37). These processes led to the revival of artisan industries in the mid-1930s. Banaras handloom silk weavers, who had faced falling demand and competition from low-priced Japanese and Chinese artificial silk during the depression, gradually switched to cheaper imported silk yarn and thus were able to produce fabrics at lower prices. Moreover, demand for specialized Banaras (sic) silk, used for social and religious ceremonies, also began to pick up and the silk industry revived quickly (ibid.: 38). During the same period, communal relations led to a new kind of antagonism. While in the 19th century Banaras, a process of polarization of Muslim and Hindu identities was taking place among the weaving communities, and by the beginning of 20th century the city witnessed rising Hindu revivalism and reform (Gould, 2002: 630).

Silk Handloom Weavers: A Study

More than 500,000 weavers live in and around Varanasi, weaving silk saris mainly for the domestic market. But since the 1990s, these silk handloom weavers have seen their markets vanish. There are many reasons for this decline: increasing competition from power-loom weaving, changes in government protection policies, rising prices in raw silk and shifts in market demand. In the past five years, as import tariffs have come down and restrictions have been lifted, imports of silk fabric from China into India have more than doubled, exacerbating the poverty of Baranasi silk weavers. The impact of increasing competition in recent years on sari weavers has been dramatic. Workers' wages have halved since the 1990s, and local traders estimate that half the weavers have shifted to other jobs such as rickshaw pulling or construction work. Many have also died from starvation or have committed suicide.

Since 1995, the demand for silk has been shrinking and 60 per cent of handlooms are idle. Lack of ownership among stakeholders is a significant bottleneck. Though the traders are making profits selling Banarasi saris, they do not seem to invest in improving production in the area. For them, running their business and getting orders is what matters most. Most of them deal in a range of textile products (power-loom products, handloom products, made-ups, etc., of both silk and non-silk yarns) and have inadequate incentive to invest in improving the handloom quality and production to regain the lost market share.

The weavers, who are the real stakeholders and take ownership of the weaving occupation, are into weaving more by compulsion than choice. Additionally, these poor weavers are cut-off from the market and are too unorganized to make any difference. They lack resources, access to market, credit and raw material, and any form of organization to have an effect on the market. The unfair trade liberalization and the bad trade politics (i.e., trade policies and trade practices), threats from the power-loom, shortage of cheap raw material, exploitation at the hands of the middlemen, lack of intellectual property rights and GI protection, changing consumer tastes and preferences, and the prevalent huge corrupt practices in the handloom cooperatives have imperilled the livelihoods of the handloom weavers.

Methodology

For the present study, the sources of data were drawn from both primary and secondary sources. The secondary sources include journals, books and literature from the internet. The present study was conducted in the city of Varanasi with a sample size of 100 respondents residing in various areas such as Rewdi Talab, Alaipur and Bazardiha. The sampling method was by stratified random sampling. The research tools used for the present survey were through interview schedule and observation method. The study is divided into three sections. The first section deals with the introduction, historical background and the crisis of weavers. The second section focuses on the socio-economic conditions of the weavers and the last section deals with the conclusions and suggestions.

Socio-economic Profile

The socio-economic profile is of immense significance in any research endeavour. It helps in thorough probing and developing deep insights into the social phenomena. The socio-economic variable provides a new direction to the entire research project thereby having a considerable impact on the entire study.

Table 4.1a

Socio-economic Profile

Age Group (in years)	*No. of Respondents*	*Percentage of Respondents*
15–25	30	30
25–35	50	50
35–45	10	10
45–55	10	10
Total	100	100

Figure 4.1

Age Group of the Weavers

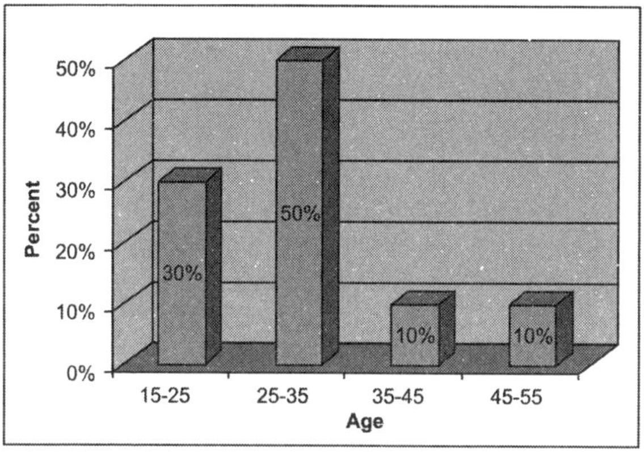

Table 4.1b

Caste Structure of the Weavers

Caste	*No. of Respondents*	*Percentage of Respondents*
General	0	0
OBC	0	0
SC	100	100
ST	0	0
Total	100	100

Figure 4.2

Caste Structure of the Weavers

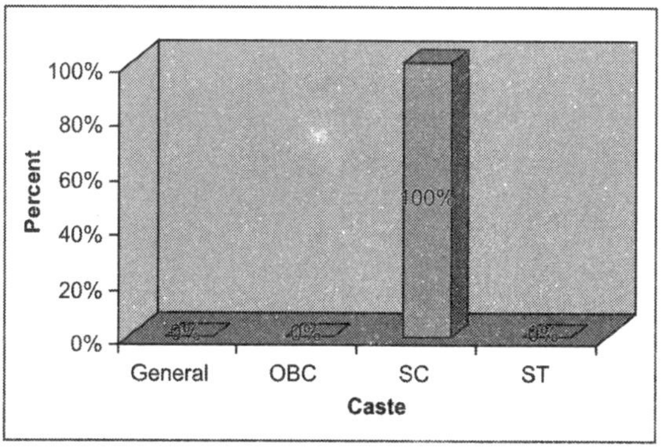

Table 4.1a clearly shows that 80 per cent of the weavers belong to 15–35 age group (youth), 10 per cent belong to 35–45 age group and rest 10 per cent belong to 45–55 age group. It is surprising that 100 per cent of the weavers belong to the Scheduled Caste (SC) category which is a reflection of the general backwardness of the weaver community (Table 4.1b). Although caste does seem to interfere in the economic process, some research suggests that while in the genesis of industrial co-operatives caste affiliations were indeed significant, such affiliations did not necessarily diffuse intra-caste differentiation in the long run.

Table 4.1c

Place of Birth of the Weavers

Place of Birth	*No. of Respondents*	*Percentage of Respondents*
In Varanasi	90	90
Out of Varanasi	10	10
Total	100	100

Table 4.1c shows that 90 per cent of the weavers belong to Varanasi and only 10 per cent are from outside the city. It is indeed a matter of great concern that in spite of a high level of technologization in the country post-globalization, the weavers are still immobile and are unable to use modern techniques in their profession. It is also a fact that in order to survive in this competitive age, one has to update oneself with the recent technology, and cost-saving and time-saving methods of production.

Table 4.1d

Educational Level of the Weavers

Education	*No. of Respondents*	*Percentage of Respondents*
Primary	40	40
Middle	20	20
High School	10	10
Illiterates	30	30
Total	100	100

Figure 4.3
Educational Level of the Weavers

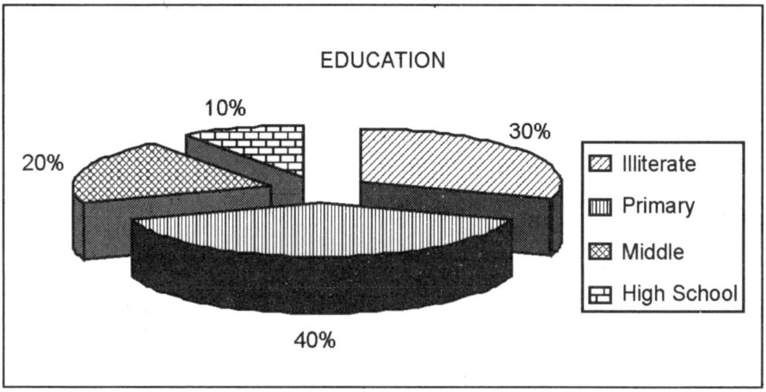

Moreover, the situation of weavers in Varanasi is even more precarious. It was found that 40 per cent of the weavers had just received primary education, 20 per cent had received education up to middle-school level and 10 per cent were high school educated. However, 30 per cent of the weavers were found to be illiterate. It becomes apparent that the majority (40% primary and 30% illiterate) of weavers are not expected to learn the modern complicated techniques of production. Even the weavers who received the maximum amount of education, i.e., up to high school are not in a position to acquire the improved skills and necessary training for the betterment of this particular sector. Due to lack of technical training, they cannot compete with many of their counterparts.

Family Structure

Despite the continuous and growing impact of urbanization, secularization and westernization, the traditional joint household, both in ideal and in practice, remains the primary social force in the lives of most Indians. Loyalty to family is a deeply held ideal for almost everyone. Joint family has continued to remain an important family structure in India.

Figure 4.4
Family Structure of the Weavers

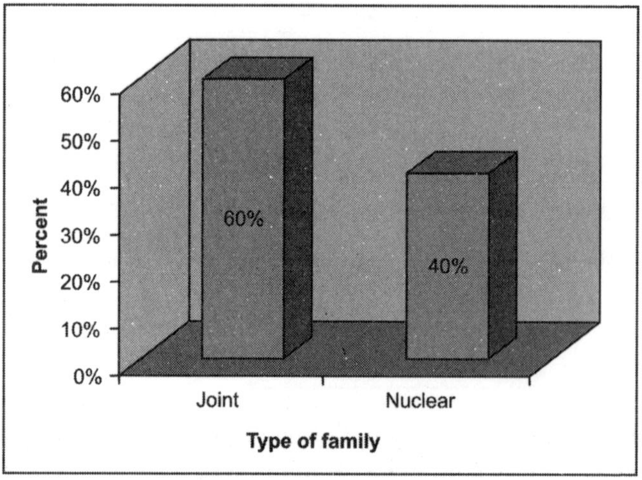

Table 4.2
Family Structure

Type of Family	*No. of Respondents*	*Percentage of Respondents*
Joint	60	60
Nuclear	40	40
Total	100	100
No. of members in the family		
0–5	0	0
5–10	50	50
10–15	30	30
15–20	20	20
Total	100	100
No. of dependents		
0–2	0	0
2–4	10	10
4–6	20	20

Cont'd...

...Cont'd

6–8	0	0
8–10	70	70
Total	100	100
Whether they have children?		
Yes	80	80
No	20	20
Total	100	100

Table 4.2 reveals that 60 per cent of the weavers were in the joint family system, while the rest 40 per cent were from nuclear families. This gives a clear picture that the majority of the weaving communities in Varanasi are from traditional backgrounds since joint family is one of the most traditional family set-ups in India. It is even believed that joint families are a reflection of the Indian culture and the transmitters of cultural values. Irawati Karve (1953) defines joint family as "a group of people who live under one roof, eat food cooked at one hearth, hold property in common, have common worship and are related to each other as some particular type of kindred". So, people in joint families are so deeply influenced by traditional family norms that they are slow to adapt to changes. Even the joint family sentiments prevailed among them acted as an obstacle in migrating to cities or even being mobile. They have thoroughly imbibed the joint family norms of living in the same house and professing the family profession. This prohibits them from not only taking up any new profession, but also from using enhanced skills to modernize their present profession. It was also found that 50 per cent of the family of weavers comprised 5–10 members, 30 per cent had 10–15 members and rest 20 per cent had 15–20 members in their family. Eighty per cent of the weavers had children and only 20 per cent did not have children as they were unmarried. It appears that since 100 per cent of the weaving populations were Muslims, therefore they were not prepared to adopt family planning methods due to the traditional orthodox nature of Islam. Further, it was found that 70 per cent of the weavers had 8–10 dependents

in their families. Twenty per cent had 4–6 dependents and the rest 10 per cent had 2–4 dependents. This shows that they are engulfed by a severe economic burden which is absorbing a large proportion of their income for consumption which could instead be used for capital formation.

Table 4.3
Education of Children

	Number of Respondents	*Percentage of Respondents*
Whether the children go to school?		
Yes	60	60
No	40	40
Total	100	100
Whether girls receive formal education?		
Yes	60	60
No	40	40
Total	100	100

Figure 4.5
Children Going to School

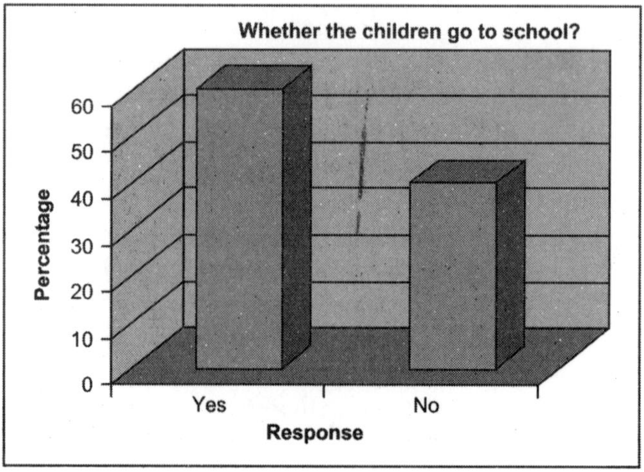

Table 4.3 reveals that 40 per cent of the children of the weavers have never been to school and 60 per cent children who go to school receive only primary education in *madrasas*. This is due to the fact that the weavers could not afford any kind of formal education which entails even a nominal fee structure due to increasing poverty among them. Therefore, they prefer to send their children to *madrasas*. It was even found that 40 per cent of the girl children were out of the educational net, while 60 per cent of the girls received formal education (primary education in *madrasas*). It was found that most of the respondents were in favour of formal education for their children (male and female child), but they could not send them to schools due to financial instability and crisis. One of the respondents remarked, "we used to send our children to school but could not send them because of the financial problem due to the heavy losses suffered in weaving as a profession". It needs no emphasis that profit is the difference between the cost of production and revenue earned. The lesser the cost, the more is the profit. The cost of production of the weavers is more as compared to the large-scale industries as they use old and outdated techniques of production. Therefore, it becomes

Figure 4.6

Formal Education for Girls

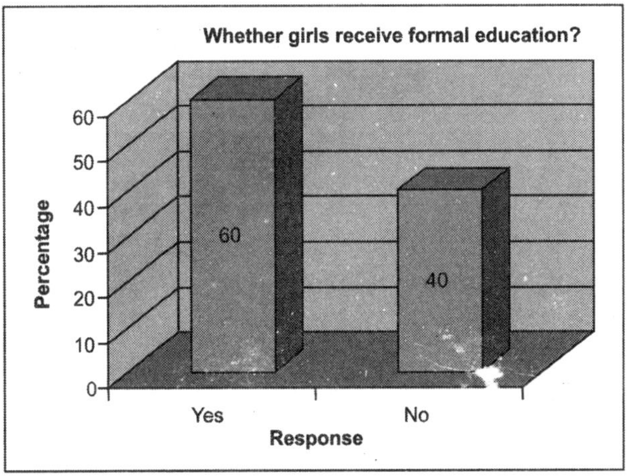

apparent that the future weavers would be unskilled as they receive only education up to the primary level. Since the weavers are unable to update their skills due to lack of proper education and technical expertise, they continue to remain in this vicious circle of poverty.

Table 4.4
Perception about Marriage

Age at Marriage (in years)	*Number of Respondents*	*Percentage of Respondents*
18–20	10	10
20–22	20	20
22–24	10	10
24–26	30	30
26 and above	10	10
Unmarried	20	20
Total	100	100
Adoption of Family Planning Methods		
Yes	70	70
No	30	30
Total	100	100

Figure 4.7
Age at Marriage

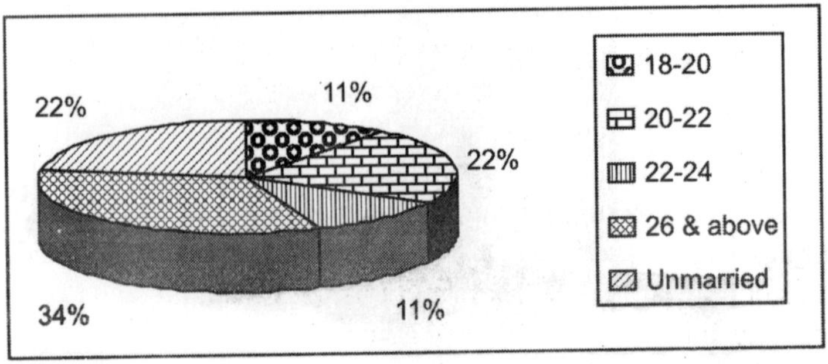

The institution of marriage occupies an important place in the Indian society. According to Hindu Marriage Act 1955, the marriageable age has been increased to 18 years for girls and 21 years for boys. Table 4.4 reveals that 34 per cent of the weavers got married at the age of 26 and above 22 per cent were married at the age of 20–22, 11 per cent were married at 18–20 and the rest 22 per cent were unmarried. Though the marriageable age has been increased from 18 to 21 years for boys, yet it was found that 11 per cent of the weavers got married at an early age (18–22), which has contributed to increased number of dependents at an early age.

Figure 4.8
Proper Age at Marriage

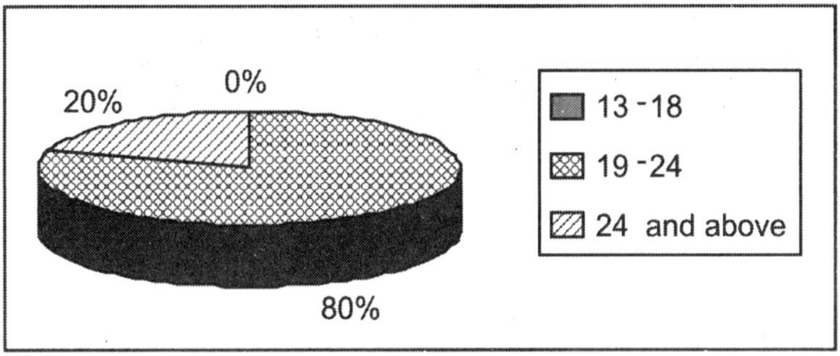

It is quite surprising that regarding proper age at marriage, 80 per cent of the respondents believed that 19–24 years is the proper age for marriage and 20 per cent of the respondents were in favour of 24 years and above age group. This clearly shows that educational backwardness has become an important factor for them to interpret the proper age of marriage. Most of the weavers get married at an early age and thereby have a number of children engaged in the same profession. Since they go through massive financial crunch, they cannot afford to send their children to schools. As a result of which more and more children adopt the profession of their fathers without updating their skills. Due to lack of training and skill among them, they continue to languish in poverty and hand to mouth existence.

Table 4.5
Availability of Credit Facilities

Preference for Taking Loans	*No. of Respondents*	*Percentage of Respondents*
Organized sector	40	40
Unorganized sector	60	60
Total	100	100
Whether they gain profits?		
Yes	10	10
No	90	90
Total	100	100

Figure 4.9
Preference for Taking Loans

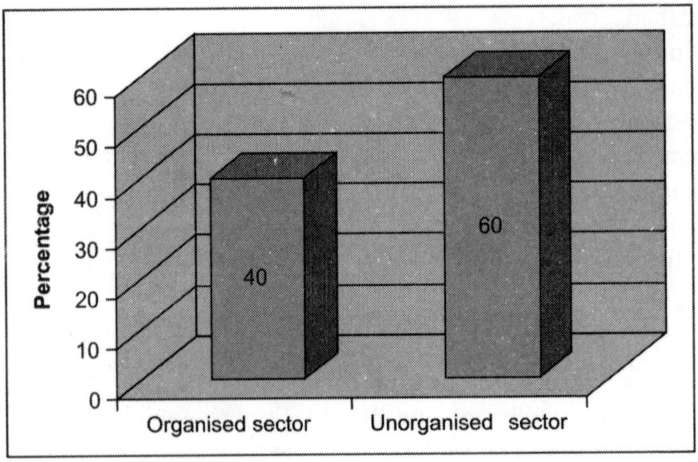

It is indeed true that finances continue to remain an important factor for the formation of capital. In case of weavers, the availability of finances would help them to enhance their skills and bring about necessary changes in their profession. But due to paucity of funds they are unable to introduce new techniques, in their profession, in order to compete in the world market. Globalization and increased automation has brought immense changes in every sector of life. In this context, it becomes apparent that the weavers should implement new modern techniques in their production in order to survive. But, it is also surprising that the weavers were not interested in taking loans.This is perhaps due to the fact that since all of them belong to the Muslim community, taking loans is not a priority. Moreover, Islam as a religion proscribes taking of loans and interests on loans. This shows that religion continues to penetrate into every sector of their life and occupies a dominant position. It was quite clear that the weavers are least interested in taking loans, but in case they would take a loan in worst circumstances, they would prefer the unorganized sector (60%).

The unorganized sector comprises of moneylenders (who charge exorbitant interest rates), traders (who purchase the finished goods at a cheaper price), commission agents (who help them to marketize their products), employers (who supply them raw silk and they in turn provide them with the finished goods at a very low wage). With regard to taking loans from the organized sector, it was revealed that only 40 per cent of the respondents preferred the organized sector. There is no denying the fact that the rate of interest varies in both the sectors. While in the organized sector, namely, banks and other financial institutions, the rate of interest was 12–13 per cent. On the contrary, in the unorganized sector, the rate of interest was 36–40 per cent.

However, it can be pointed out that in case they take loans from traders, they (weavers) have to supply goods at a very low price and in case loans are provided by the employers, they get lower wages in turn. In this way in any case, the weaver is exploited to the extent that on one side their revenue is not increasing due to the causes mentioned above, and on the other side they are not able to use modern cost-saving techniques of production. It needs no emphasis that the difference between the revenue and the cost is called profit. Since the revenue does not increase and they are not able to curtail the cost, the chance of gaining profits is dismal.

Table 4.6

Future Prospects of Weaving as a Profession

Whether They Aspire for the Next Generation to Adopt Weaving as a Profession?	*Number of Respondents*	*Percentage of Respondents*
Yes	10	10
No	90	90
Total	100	100
Number of Members in the Weaving Profession in the Family		
0–2	30	30
2–4	60	60
4–8	0	0
8–10	10	10
Total	100	100
Hours of Work per Day		
0–5	0	0
5–10	90	90
10–15	10	10
Total	100	100
Whether They are Interested for Any Other Profession?		
Yes	90	90
No	10	10
Total	100	100

Figure 4.10

Whether they aspire the next generation to adopt weaving?

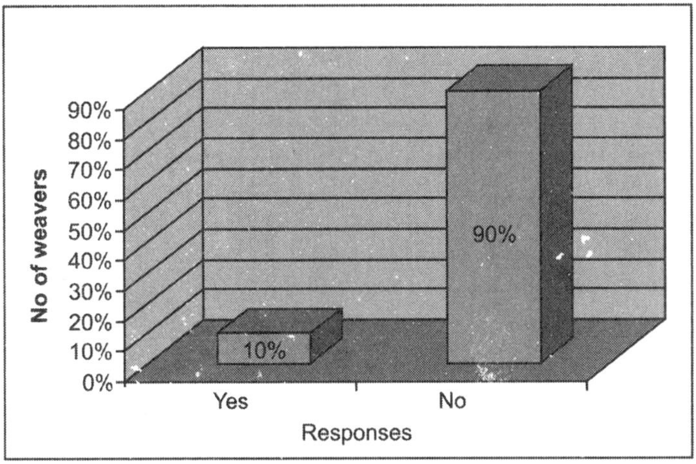

The above figure clearly shows that 90 per cent of the respondents were not interested for their next generation to adopt weaving a as profession. The rest 10 per cent felt that they were unable to provide facilities for the upliftment of the future generation so they had to resort to the same profession.

Figure 4.11

Whether they are interested in any other profession?

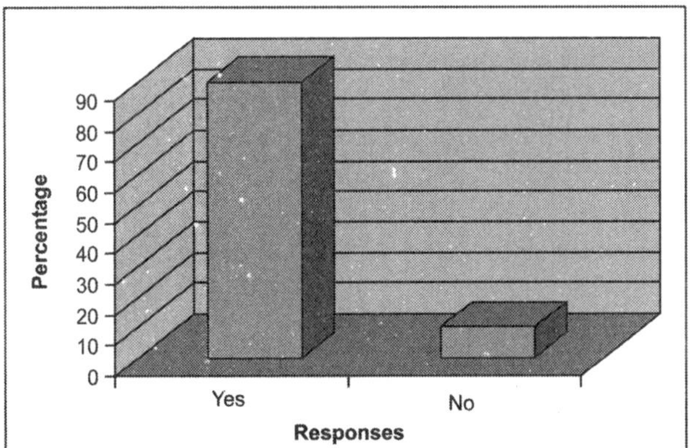

From the above diagram it is revealed that 90 per cent of the respondents were not interested in the same profession (weaving), while the rest 10 per cent felt that they were not educated enough to change their profession, so they had to continue with weaving as a profession.

From Figure 4.10 it is revealed that majority of the weavers (90%) did not aspire their future generation to adopt weaving as a profession, while 10 per cent were not interested, but they had to do weaving out of compulsion. This is perhaps due to the perpetual backwardness of their profession. The weavers, being unskilled, are unable to update their skills and make new improvements in their profession in order to meet the demands of the market. Therefore, they are pushed down and languish in poverty. Due to poverty and general backwardness, they are unable to afford education for their children in good schools. But they would want that their children should not join the same profession rather should be educated and be socially mobile for any better occupation in the society. But out of no choice they had to adopt weaving for their next generation. It is even interesting to find that 60 per cent of the respondents replied that at least 2–4 members of their family were engaged in weaving as a profession. Thirty per cent had at least 0–4 people in the family engaged in weaving as a profession and 10 per cent had 8–10 members in their family engaged in weaving. This clearly shows that weaving had become a family profession among the weavers. Moreover, it is a dominant mode of occupation for almost all of them.

With regard to hours of work, 90 per cent of weavers said that they work for 5–10 hours per day, whereas the rest 10 per cent work for 10–15 hours per day. Since there is a situation of power crisis in Uttar Pradesh, their productivity depends on the availability of electricity. But it is a sad state of affairs that their work is completely dependent on electricity and they cannot work for longer hours due to frequent power cuts in Varanasi.

With regard to their interest for any other profession, 90 per cent of the weavers agreed that given an opportunity, they would definitely change their profession. According to a rough estimate, around 60 per cent of the weavers have abandoned their traditional occupation and have either migrated to cities in search of livelihoods as unskilled labourers or have become rickshaw-pullers or brick-kiln workers. The rest 10 per cent replied in the negative since they were aware of the fact that they were not skilled enough to compete for any other job due to lack of education. So, they preferred to continue with weaving as a profession.

Conclusion

There is no denying the fact that the crisis among the weavers of Varanasi is continuing to deteriorate their condition. The weavers in Varanasi are in a constant state of financial burden which has made their social life even more deplorable. The above study was an attempt to understand and interpret the present socio-economic conditions of weavers of Varanasi. In the study, it was revealed that half of the respondents belong to the age group of 25–35 (youth). With Indian youth becoming a powerful demographic entity; they are the major propellers of social change. Therefore, it becomes imperative to inculcate in them proper skills and measures for upliftment so that they are able to compete in the world market in this age of globalization. It was revealed that most of the weavers belonged to the joint family set-up with large number of dependents in the family. With increase in the number of family members and accompanying heavy economic burden, the drop-out rate of the children increased.

However, with regard to developmental schemes for the upliftment of weavers, the success rate is not high and more attention needs to be given to this sector. There are developmental schemes such as government subsidies and protective measures including reservation of 11 varieties of cloth for the handloom sector. Credit and marketing support by the government includes cash credit assistance at concessional rates to primary co-operatives and state-level apex bodies. Credit allocations across the states and districts are highly skewed and are based on very little verification of credit requirements. There is much evidence of bogus co-operatives that have cornered a large share of government credit. Government modernization schemes have included the promotion of frame looms and jacquard looms, training to weavers in new techniques. There are several drawbacks with frame looms that the weavers have identified themselves such as less flexibility, having to weave in worksheds as opposed to in the house, more physically difficult and substantial additional investment expenses which weavers cannot afford.

The Indian government has also initiated many developmental programmes and welfare schemes for weavers. For example, the Handloom Development Centres Schemes introduced in 1993, the Handloom Village Development Scheme, the Workshed-cum-Housing Scheme and the Thrift-cum-Savings scheme. It is hard to differentiate one government scheme from another as their goals are vague and they lack clearly defined priorities. They also seem to be devised by New Delhi and implemented at the state level without much reference to regional specificities or requirements. Other schemes include distribution of credit cards by commercial banks to the weavers. Allahabad Bank has decided to extend the facility to silk weavers in and around Varanasi. The idea behind the move is to save weavers from perennial exploitation by moneylenders. About 200 weavers were identified for the first round of the scheme that was implemented in Varanasi, Azamgarh, Mirzapur, Chandauli and Sant Kabir Nagar districts of the poverty-ridden eastern Uttar Pradesh.

In spite of these plethora of governmental measures, the need is to create and promote structures that organize the weavers to collectively engage with the market; provide them with quality raw materials and other facilities; and consequently, enhancing their bargaining power in the production process. Initiating, identifying and promoting such existing organizations should be given the greatest priority.

References

Gooptu, Nandini. *The Politics of Urban Poor in Early Twentieth Century India*. Cambridge: Cambridge University Press, 2001.

Gould, William. "Congress Radicals and Hindu Militancy: Sampurnanand and Purushottam Das Tandon in the Politics of the United Provinces, 1930–1947", *Modern Asian Studies* 36 (3), 2002: 619–55.

Karve, I. *Kinship Organisation in India*. Poona: Deccan College, 1953.

Kumar, Nita. *The Artisans of Banaras: Popular Culture and Identity, 1880–1986*. Princeton: Princeton University Press, 1988.

——. "Work and Leisure in the Formation of Identity: Muslim Weavers in a Hindu City", in *Culture and Power in Banaras: Community, Performance and Environment, 1800–1980*, ed. Sandria B. Freitag, Berkeley: University of California Press, 1989, 147–70.

Pandey, B.P. *Banaras Brocades: Structure and Functioning*. Varanasi: Gandhian Institute of Studies, 1981.

Pandey, Gyanendra. *The Construction of Communalism in Colonial North India*. Delhi: Oxford University Press, 1990.

Showeb, M. *Silk Handloom Industry in Varanasi: A Study of Socio-Economic Problems of Weavers*. Varanasi: Ganga Kaveri Publishing House, 1994.

Part II

GLOBALIZATION AND SOCIO-CULTURAL CHANGE

5

Globalization, Technology and Changing Youth Culture in India

A Sociological Perspective

Ellina Samantroy

The unprecedented growth in the number of young people in the world today can be characterized as one of the crucial reality factors conditioning political and cultural developments. There is no denying the fact that the youth comprise the largest demographic entity in India and are identified as major propellers of social change. With social change accelerating due to the onset of globalization, religious values of the youth have undergone tremendous change.

Young people across the world are looking for alternatives and seek deeper understanding of the nature of man and society. They are open to imaginative insights that might lead to a more humane future. Cultural relations widen the range in which man lives his life, including working out the relationships of means and ends, technology and social purpose and one set of cultural goals to another. The youth today are to a considerable degree social activists in reacting to their own social situation. At the same time, the values of many youth represent personal philosophies that have been abandoned elsewhere, particularly as they relate to the inner world. But, a current dilemma for the contemporary society in its relationship with young people is how to continue to espouse cultural values which appear dysfunctional to the youth. In recent times, because of increasing confusion evident in educational, political and social thinking surrounding youth and their transition to adulthood, there have been suggestions that a specific statement of social goals for youth needs to be made explicit and also a related set of policy and strategy must be constructed.

When it comes to youth using technology, the unease is often stronger than the enthusiasm. Today's youth is often portrayed as self-centred, lacking in social values. They are also sometimes described as cynical, angry, violent and self-absorbed. The questions often outweigh the answers. Is youth really benefiting from their use of digital media? Can this technology truly improve the process of learning? Does it lead to dumbing youth and misfocusing our educational efforts? Is technology responsible for the stress of youth which in turn leads to a "violent generation"? These questions are just a sampling of the widespread concerns raised not just by cynics, moralists and technophobes, but also by sensible and well-meaning people. What are the fears of the new generation? What is happening to our youth? While there is much to be learned about many real dangers that warrant good management on the part of business people, educators, parents and lawmakers, investigations and surveys indicate that the cynics, technophobes and moralists are dead wrong. Today's youth is learning, developing and thriving in the digital world. They need better tools, better access, more services and more freedom to explore, not the opposite. Rather than hostility and mistrust on the part of adults, we, especially parents, educators, lawmakers, etc., need a change in our thinking and behaviour.

Many people describe youth today as materialistic, self-absorbed, cynical and demanding immediate gratification. While this generation contains many differing classes, races, religions and social perspectives, some common themes are emerging. They are the young navigators who are in constant search for a new kind of identity. They doubt that traditional institutions can provide them with good life and take personal responsibility for their lives. They do value material goods but they are not self-absorbed. They are more knowledgeable than any previous generation and they care deeply about social issues. They strongly believe in individual rights such as privacy and rights to information. But they have no ethos of individualism. Rather, they thrive from close interpersonal networks and displaying a strong sense of social responsibility. They appear very determined and even optimistic about the future, but are unsettled about difficulties facing them. Those who believe that these youth will be passive supporters of the status quo is really surprising?

The advent of globalization and heightened consumerism has led to an erosion of old values and culture patterns surrounding the personality development of the modern youth. Robertson (1992) stresses the fact that while modernization accelerates globalization, globalization is a distinct process. However, the inescapable momentum of the 20th century technology has made globalization far more obvious, thanks to the interconnected systems of economic exchange, transportation and communications. Perhaps the key shift in the late 20th century has been people's newfound consciousness of globalization, resulting in "global reflexivity": a heightened awareness of "cultural others" and diverse images of the world, resulting in a sharpened awareness of multiculturalism and indigenous, cultural, moral and religious identities (Osmer, 1999).

Globalization, however, does not just claim youth for the sake of cultural identity; it claims them because it wants something from them: consumption. The tension, of course, lies in the fact that while it may be in globalization's best interest to socialize adolescents into the norms of the global community, it is in the adolescents' best interest to resist those norms until they can freely choose, and until the social roles and skills necessary for survival in a global culture (including the skills of rhetorical discernment, reflection and evaluation) can be mastered. This tension represents what Meyer and Geschiere (1999) call the "fix and flux" inherent to identity formation, and the cultural surround represents a given community's symbolic resources for negotiating a balance between the two. Traditionally, "fix" went without saying: where we lived, what our vocation would be, the roles we would assume in our communities were, basically, given. "Youth" were often characterized by radical flux because so many borders of self – from national identity to sexual orientation – were already established by the society in which they lived. Meyer and Geschiere (ibid.) further point out that globalization inverts that equation: "flux" is the normative state of the global surrounds, and this "unmooring of identity" leads us to grab anxiously, prematurely and uncritically at "fix" wherever we can find it. One result of these "unmoored identities" has been a resurgence of highly differentiated and often rigidly and arbitrarily defined people groups who "fix" their borders in opposition to cultural "others" (which, in the global situation, is a little like defining your location in relationship to a moving target).

In the sociological and post-modern literature, "youth" is conceptualized as relational, as "social processes whereby age is socially constructed, institutionalized and controlled in historically and culturally specific ways" (Wyn and White, 1997: 11). However, youth is still often idealized and institutionalized as a deficit state of "becoming" that exists and has meaning in relation to the "adult" it will "arrive" to be. Structures play a role in the governance of the society in general and in particular for youth, but the impact of agency, the capacity for acting intentionally in our modern world need to be acknowledged so the politico-socio-economic contexts in which youth exist need to be understood (ibid.). While the physical and psychological changes that occur in youth are important, the way these are constructed by the society and in turn negotiated by individuals is equally important. Youth, in all ages, has been in the vanguard of progress and social change. Thirst for freedom, impatience for quicker pace of progress and a passion for innovation, coupled with idealism and creative fervour, saw the youth in the forefront of the freedom struggle in our own land. If our youth was inspired by the call of the Father of the Nation in the first half of this century, the youth of today face the challenge of economic development and technological progress with social justice.

The youth of India, representing a third of our population, constitute a vital and vibrant human resource. They have a right, as well as an obligation, to participate actively in national development and in shaping the destiny of the nation which is, in fact, their own destiny. Their problems are many and varied, and their aspirations naturally high, in a country with a great past and greater promise for the future. The need, therefore, is to create increasing opportunities for them to develop their personality and their functional capability, and thus make them economically productive and socially useful. Therefore, in this paper, I have tried to unravel the emerging cultural traits and values with regard to the major social institutions such as family and marriage among the Indian youth under diversified social situations and cultural contexts.

Hybridized Youth: Youth Culture in Post-modern Era

There are a host of paradoxes and contradictions in the globalization process – an uneven process that is not simply about global extent or infrastructure beyond national borders. But it may also be about the functional density of interactions of worldwide systems. There may be global convergence around some features or global dispersion or diffusion from a local phenomenon. While some elements seem interlinked and possibly even tending to the universal – global markets, commodification, consumption, the Internet, international fashion and various integrated world systems – there are also multiple cultural, ethnic, language, political, historical, economic, ideological and social differences. While it can both narrow and widen the income gaps between and within nations, it can diminish, yet may also intensify, political domination, and lead to both homogeneity as well as pluralized cultural identities. Globalization favours some groups and some countries, while threatening others. It has a strong Anglo-European bias that economically disadvantages the developing world (Stiglitz, 2002). As a result, where globalized economic changes make people disadvantaged, displaced and/or unemployed, there is often emergence of right-wing, fundamentalist ideas that promise a return to old values and certainties, in turn, destabilizing such societies with civil unrest, violence and possibly war. Yet, the paradox is not entirely negative, as Krause (2002) points out that

> trade liberalization destroys rural societies as well as the environment, weakens the labour movement, and threatens cultural diversity and self-determination ... [however] technology is providing a communications forum for organizations and individuals that are generally ignored – or stereotyped in negative terms – by the corporate-controlled mainstream media. By giving these organizations a voice, technology is increasing the likelihood that their concerns will be acknowledged, and – hopefully – addressed.

Globalization and post-modernity are inextricably intertwined with notions of a consumer society and commodification. Post-modern approaches tend to emphasize the dual cultural processes of constructing youth identity, through the market, as an aspect of the culture of advanced consumerism and through the agency of youth themselves. The categorization of youth, in relation to the market – be it the young cosmetics and beauty market, the youth fashion market or the latest music fad – is highlighted as a socio-cultural construction based on the concept of style and lifestyle, with an emphasis on what Foucault (1965) called the "aesthetics of existence". Foucault pointed out how over time, through discourse, we continually devise categories and norms that specify, position and define people in different ways, e.g., the insane, mad, fools, childhood, adolescence, nuclear family, extended family, etc. Childhood and the family are constructed as cultural artefacts. Historically, economic changes have caused social and cultural upheavals and even moral panic, yet have also led to the construction and definition of new identities. But post-modernism is not simply a re-formulation of identities and new narratives in terms of social constructionism (Gergen, 2001).

Post-modernism involves a different way of thinking, of considering discourses, cultural practices and power relations, and of considering sites where new kinds of identities are constructed. In the post-modern era, we see new gender roles, new identities, new cultural practices, new family configurations and new emerging communities. Many of these things are a direct response to the ability to network or communicate globally via the Internet. Bauman (1992) would rightly argue that "postmodernity's most conspicuous features are variety, contingency and ambivalence, and the permanent and irreducible pluralism of cultures, communal traditions, ideologies, forms of life, language games". Post-modern approaches tend to hold that the self is socially constructed in the post-modern, globalized era, and from the viewpoint of the market, youth are consummate consumers. Now, more than ever, youth find their identities and values in the marketplace, rather than in traditional sources such as family, church, educational institutions that comprise a locality, and moreover that marketplace is an increasingly globalized one. Giroux (1990) warns that while

> youth may be experiencing the indeterminacy, senselessness, and multiple conditions of postmodernism, but corporate advertizers are attempting to theorize pedagogy of consumption as part of a new campaign to appropriate postmodern differences among youth across racial, class, gender and sexual lines. The lesson to be learned from the market's approach to multiculturalism is that differences among youth matter politically and pedagogically, but not simply as a way of generating new markets or registering difference as a fashion index.

Since post-modernism is the logic of late capitalism, where the culture of consumption has taken over from the culture of production, when we talk about youth in the post-modern era we need to think in terms of them consuming their identities in the global marketplace. In what way could youth be considered to be "hybridized"? The notion of hybridization as it applies to youth in the post-modern era refers to their negotiation of the local and the global and the intrusion, imposition and inter-connected ess of these spatial and cultural locations. They make individual choices that are reinforced by a market logic that creates them as niche markets and thus the market logic of the post-modern condition has the effect of manufacturing, legitimating and then exploiting their identity/subjectivities. With the emergence of new cultural hybridity, many young people may identify themselves as cultural or ethnic blends with multiple identities such as British-Pakistani-Muslim or Indo-American-Canadian.

With globalization, the world is becoming increasingly interconnected, with simultaneous pressures towards, paradoxically, both unity and diversity. One of the major factors in the diversification of youth cultures is the rate at which cultural objects and ideas are transmitted throughout the world, for when communities are cut off from technologies that can disseminate information and ideas widely, there appears to be much less diversity. In societies where social change is slow or resisted, becoming adult remains in a similar, traditional, expected and familiar pattern for each generation. Rapid social change alters this. The old, familiar patterns of the past and those that the parents had undergone no longer fit once the social context has changed. Adults often find it difficult to help the young to negotiate a smooth transition to adulthood (Griswold, 2006). In what adults often view as something negative or rebellious, youth search for new and relevant identities, once they realize that they cannot learn from past experiences. Youth produce their identities and cultures from images and ideas they receive from the media and new technology.

Post-modern youth cultures are emerging due to the impact of globalization, the mass media and information technology, rather than simply as a result of the processes of marginalization or alienation. Giroux (1990) argues that the new information and communication technologies, through emphasizing individualism, creates both a sense of alienation and of boredom with school which can no longer compete with such exciting technology. Yet through the impact of globalizing effects of information technology, post-modern marketing, consumerism and mass media, adolescent perceptions, expectations and experiences in many countries are linked and sometimes become homogenized such that a post-modern youth culture is, arguably, emerging.

According to Arnett (2002), there are four major issues related to identity, which develop due to globalization. The first is the development of a bicultural identity or perhaps a hybrid identity, which means that part of one's identity is rooted in the local culture, while another part stems from an awareness of one's relation to the global world. The development of global identities is no longer just a part of immigrants and ethnic minorities. People today especially the young, develop an identity that gives them a sense of belonging to a worldwide culture, which includes an awareness of events, practices, styles and information that are a part of the global culture. Media such as television and especially the Internet which allows instant communication at any place in the world, play an important part in developing a global identity. Yet along with this new global identity, people continue to retain and develop their local identity for daily interactions with their family, friends and community. A good example of bicultural identity is among the educated youth in India who despite being integrated into the global fast-paced technological world, may continue to have deep-rooted traditional Indian values with respect to their personal lives and choices such as preference for an arranged marriage, caring for parents in their old age. Although developing a bicultural identity means that a local identity is retained alongside a global identity, there is no doubt that local cultures are being modified by globalization. As traditional cultural practices and beliefs change, a bicultural or a hybrid multicultural identity likely develops to include the elements of the native, local and global culture.

The second issue is identity confusion which individuals from non-western cultures experience as a response to globalization. While people may adapt to changes and develop bicultural or hybrid and multicultural identities, some may find it difficult to adapt to rapid changes. The ways of the global culture may seem out of reach, too foreign or even undermining their own cultural values and beliefs. Instead of becoming bicultural, they may feel isolated and excluded from both their local culture and the global culture, truly belonging to neither. Identity confusion among young people may be reflected in problems such as depression, suicide and substance abuse. A variety of cultures have experienced a sharp increase in suicide and substance abuse among their young people, since their rapid move towards joining the global culture.

The third change brought about by globalization is the growth of the self-selected culture which means people choose to form groups with like-minded persons who wish to have an identity that is untainted by the global culture and its values. The values of the global culture, which are based on individualism, free market economics and democracy, and include freedom of choice, individual rights, openness to change and tolerance to differences are part of "western values". For most people worldwide, what the global culture has to offer is appealing.

The fourth consequence of globalization is the spread of emerging adulthood. The timing of transitions to adult roles such as work, marriage and parenthood are occurring at later stages in most parts of the world as the need for preparing for jobs in an economy that is highly technological and information-based is slowly extending from the late teens to the mid-20s. Additionally, as the traditional hierarchies of authority weaken and break down under the pressure of globalization, the youth are forced to develop control over their own lives including marriage and parenthood. The spread of emerging adulthood is related to issues of identity. Where a period of emerging adulthood is present, young people have a longer period for identity explorations in love and work before they commit themselves to long-term choices. By experiencing different love relationships, different educational possibilities and different jobs, they learn more about themselves, and they clarify their preferences and abilities. Emerging adulthood is possible only in societies where economic development is high enough that the labour of young people is not urgently needed. They are allowed to spend their late teens and early to mid-20s exploring possibilities for self-development because there is no pressing need for them to contribute to the economic well-being of their families

(Arnett, 2002). Appadurai (1996) argues that modern technologies of communication across the boundaries of real time and real space in social interactions and "virtual communities" or groups may be possible, but it does not overcome the acuteness of crisis of cultural identities.

Social and Cultural Impact of Globalization on Family and Marriage

The Indian society is drastically changing as a result of globalization. India traditionally has followed the joint-family system. Contemporary changes are taking place in the institution of family, and the nuclear-family system is increasingly the norm. So far, the concept of single parenthood has not caught on in the Indian culture. However, divorce rates are increasing. Urbanization, at times, has seen changes and this in turn has brought about a lot of changes in the Indian culture. Many marriages are breaking up for many reasons, such as modern lifestyles, professional ambitions and unrealistic expectations. Commitment for marriage is disappearing as a result of modernization in India now (*India Today*, 1 August 1998, under section called "Marriages" by Sheela Raval, *Till Whims Do Us Part*: 60–61). In cities, young people are starting to choose their own partners. Arranged marriages, however, are still there. The upper-class and middle-class people of India and the urban Indians have changed a lot in their cultural values as a result of the impact of information technology and media.

Consumerism has permeated and changed the fabric of the contemporary Indian society. The study of families and changes they experience as a system although rich and complex can be very time consuming and expensive, and perhaps best obtained in one family at a time through clinical counters. However, the study of social changes is extensive and often supports the impact of changes in families. Fragmentation of the traditional family network is leading to an erosion of the available support within the immediate and extended family. Migration of younger generations from rural to urban areas and from one urban centre to another as well as transnational migration has resulted in the elderly being left to fend for themselves at a time when family support becomes more crucial. With more women joining the workforce system, care of the aged within families has declined. For those who live within extended families, the elderly have to live in harmony with the younger generation that has to face a highly competitive world of globalization. While the nuclear family system is increasingly becoming the norm, modern lifestyles, changing professional and personal expectations are impacting relationships of marriage and commitment. In cities, young people are exploring new relationships which are completely alien to Indian culture. Live-in relationships are increasing in cities and the youngsters are not giving importance to the institution of marriage.

We now live in an increasingly networked society which involves more and more mobility; while social relationships are characterized by distance created through new technology; physical travel has become an increasingly important glue for the survival of these relationships. Virtual contact goes hand in hand with physical contact, so although the information revolution has introduced new "virtual" ways of travelling, physical mobility has simultaneously increased. Thus, those societies with most advanced forms of new communication tend to have high levels of physical travel, so electronic networks are generating more not less global contact (Urry, 2003). The impact of information technology has made it possible to create "virtual interaction", as Appadurai has rightly suggested, which leads to the erosion of real, intimate means of communication and creation of a social relationship involving values and sentiments.

With heightened consumerism and the lure for a highly materialistic life, the techno-savvy youth value commodities more than relationships. The highly competitive information society makes them more ambitious in order to adapt to the rapid changes. Such a condition makes them ignore personal relationships at the cost of maintaining their professional ethics. While trying to adapt themselves to the multicultural realities, the youth are somehow quite perplexed about constructing their own identity.

Conclusion

Therefore, it can be argued that globalization has ushered in many technological, economic and social changes among the youth in

India which affect their traditional cultural styles, forms and ideologies. As a consequence of globalization and the advent of a pluralistic culture, the challenges of creating a viable identity are perhaps greater than they have been in the past. According to (1991), "when globalization alters and erodes traditional ways, identity has to be created and recreated on a more active basis than before". Identity is less influenced by prescribed social roles and based more on individual choices, on decisions that each person makes about what values to embrace and what paths to pursue in love and work. Some people react to this responsibility with identity confusion or seek refuge in a self-selected culture that offers more structure and takes over some decisions.

It can be argued that the process of globalization, mass media and information technology have been instrumental in creation of postmodern youth cultures. The globalizing effects of new information and communication technology cannot be ignored since they have created a homogenization of adolescent perceptions, expectations and experiences in many countries and led to the emergence of a postmodern youth culture. Postmodernism is often considered the logic of late capitalism where the culture of consumption plays a vital role than the culture of production. When one speaks of youth in postmodern era, he/she has to consider consuming their identities in a global marketplace. Youth will often blend different sub-cultural styles through an active, creative, hybridizing process which produces a new product from pre-formed materials, but generally does not invent new cultural and aesthetic resources per se. Rather than seeing youth as simply pawns of the media – that they are powerless to control, we need to urgently acknowledge youth agency. Such agency becomes apparent in the positive, constructive way that the youth select from their cultural/ethnic backgrounds and from the media those images and ideas that they want to use in constructing an identity, in creating or constituting themselves (Cagle, 1995). Therefore, Bauman would predict pluralism of cultures. It becomes a necessary task for the youth to learn to live and experience this global culture instead of being confused with their individual identities. The social effect of new technology is both instrumental and symbolic-intrinsic. At the instrumental level, it contributes to differentiation of occupations, roles and values which form a part of uniform global sub-culture, and yet in the symbolic-intrinsic domain, they endanger identities of self-consciousness that are segmentary or self-emancipating (Singh, 2000). In this context, it can be said that modern youth need to see beyond the differences of a global multicultural identity and have a shared understanding of the complex interplay of the various forces of globalization and technology. At this juncture, it becomes important to evolve a distinctive way of seeing and experiencing the social reality amidst multiple realities, and develop an understanding to appreciate the unity behind a plethora of differences.

It can be said that in this cultural matrix of the global as well as the local, homogenizing and diversifying influences continuously merge in the lifestyles, performances and everyday lives of contemporary youth. Therefore, the youth should learn to reflect on their social reality and at the same time enrich their culture by involving themselves in the process of a more mature cross-cultural understanding.

References

Appadurai, A. *Modernity at Large: Cultural Dimensions of Globalisation.* Minnepolis: University of Minnesota Press, 1996.

Arnett, J. *The Consumer Society: Myths and Structures.* London: Sage Publications, 2002.

Bauman, Z. *Intimations of Post-modernity.* London: Routledge, 1992.

Cagle, V.M. *Reconstructing Pop/Subculture: Art, Rock, and Andy Warhol.* Thousand Oaks, CA: Sage Publications, 1995.

Foucault, M. *Madness and Civilization: A History of Insanity in the Age of Reason.* London: Routledge, 1965.

Gergen, K.J. *Social Construction in Context.* London: Sage Publications, 2001.

Giddens, A. *Modernity and Self-Identity*. Cambridge: Polity Press, 1991.

Giroux, H.A. *Curriculum Discourse as Postmodern Critical Practice*. Geelong: Deakin University Press, 1990.

Griswold, W. *Cultures and Societies in a Changing World*. Thousand Oaks: Pine Forge Press, 2006.

Hall, S. and T. Jefferson, eds. *Resistance through Rituals: Youth Subcultures in Post-War Britain*. London: Hutchinson, 1976.

Krause, A. 'Hybridised World Kids: Youth Cultures in Post Modern Era'. Tina Besley. Paper presented at the European Conference on Educational Research. University of Lisbon. 11–14 September, 2002 (accessed from http://www.leeds.ac.uk/educol/documents/00002362.htm, in July 2005)

Meyer, Birgit and Peter Geschiere, eds. *Globalisation and Identity: Dialectics of Flow and Closure*. Oxford and Malden, MA: Blackwell, 1999.

Osmer, Richard R. The Teaching Ministry in a Multicultural World, unpublished paper, 1999.

Riggs, Fred W. Globalization: Key Concepts, 2002. http://www2.hawaii. edu/~fredr/glocon.htm. Accessed July 2002.

Robertson, R. *Globalisation: Social Theory and Global Culture*. Thousand Oaks, CA: Sage, 1992.

Singh, Y. *Culture Change in India: Identity and Globalisation*. Jaipur: Rawat Publications, 2000.

Stiglitz, J. *Globalisation and its Discontents*. London: Allen Lane, 2002.

Urry, J. "Social Networks: Travel and Talk", *British Journal of Sociology* 54 (2), 2003: 155–75.

Wyn, J. and R. White. *Rethinking Youth*. London: Sage Publications, 1997.

6

Locating Indian Women in the Context of Cultural Globalization

Changes and Possibilities

Ellina Samantroy

The advent of globalization has considerably affected the social life in India. Though globalization has made deep inroads into various sectors of life, yet its impact on women cannot be denied. There is no denying the fact that women constitute almost half of India's population, therefore it becomes imperative to understand the impact of globalization on such a significant section of the population who are major propellers of social change. According to the latest United Nations Development Programme (UNDP) report, India's position in the world on the parameter of Gender-related Development Index (GDI) which was 128 in 1998 has improved to 108 out of 143 countries ranked in 2000. By globalization we simply mean that the world has become more and more easily accessible and open to any one of us. This process has made the modern nations and communities increasingly more interdependent, susceptible to the market forces and flexible to the changing currents. Almost every one of us is aware that there is no escape, however strong our resistance might be, from the all too powerful clutch of globalization. For some people, it has become a craze; for others it is just fashion. But for the unaware multitude of Indian masses, it is just a distant dream or rather just a magic word. For another group, it is a new world of avenues opening up through the IT boom and for some others, it is an alternative route for progress and development through liberalized trade and corporate finance. Any way, it enhances the levels and volumes of global interaction. "Global interaction, rather than insulated isolation, has been the basis of economic progress in the world. Trade, along with migration, communication, and dissemination of scientific and technical knowledge, has helped to break the dominance of rampant poverty and the pervasiveness of 'nasty, brutish and short' lives that characterized the world. And yet, despite all the progress, life is still severely nasty, brutish and short for a large part of the world population. The great rewards of globalized trade have come to some, but not to others" (Sen, 2002).

Globalization is associated with rapid and significant human changes. Although not an entirely new phenomenon, the globalization process in the 19th century has led to promotion of international trade and investments, mostly centred on advanced industrial capitalist economies. Consequences of the global economic integration are seen to be spreading over a wide range of non-economic spheres of life all over the world. It is commonly understood as a process that rapidly transforms an otherwise disparate and heterogeneous world into a compressed, but not necessarily homogenous, entity and yet at the same time it "intensifies consciousness of the world as a whole" (Robertson, 1992: 8). If modernization is a special kind of social change which is anchored in the centrality of rationality and scientific knowledge, then globalization is that social change which supplants modernity with globality (Albrow, 1996). It has necessitated the recognition of the centrality of speed of communication in the constitution of social orders. It has given a new meaning to the concepts of "distance", "reality", "identities", "intimacy", "borders" and "barriers" (Bauman, 1998). As a consequence, "globalization" deserves to be recognized as a key idea in the context of understanding social change in human societies in contemporary times (Giddens, 1990; Waters, 1995). It is also significant to note that the new information and communication technologies have made qualitative differences in the nature and pace of human interactions across the world as well as in their own cultural zones and localities.

As for women, the impact of globalization has been interesting. On one hand, it has allowed women to become a larger part of the workforce, with opportunities for higher pay raising their self-confidence and independence. Globalization has provided a power to uproot the traditional views about women that have kept them economically poor and socially exploited. The growth of the computer and technology sector has provided middle-class educated women with better wages, flex-timings and the capacity to negotiate their role and status within the household and society. On the other hand, women continue to work in poorly paid, mentally and physically unhealthy, and insecure situations. For most women, their domestic responsibilities are not alleviated. Wage gaps have not showed any significant changes in most employment sectors other than information technology. Additionally, prostitution, abuse and dowry-related suicides are on the increase despite globalization, and some say that the materialistic greed is one of the main causes. Globalization is a double-edged process as far as women are concerned. On the one hand, majority of the women in India and other developing countries find themselves stripped off the benefit of social security, government subsidy protection of labour rights and safety nets. On the other hand, there are possibilities of better education facilities and opportunities at the transnational sense which are very attractive to the privileged few. It is however necessary to understand that effective development requires full integration of women in the development process as agents of change as well as beneficiaries because Indian women can be utilized as development resources in many ways. Symington (2002) noted that "it is selective and uneven with some boundaries falling while others are being fortified. Its impacts are felt in innumerable ways by various groups of people in different regions of the world". The globalization process has brought an increased opportunity for communication and for connecting people across boundaries, however not everyone can enjoy these means of communication. Widespread disparities still exist between women who have access and opportunities and those who do not.

This paper tries to give an overview of the challenges that Indian women are facing in this process of globalization and significant changes associated with women due to this major change in the new socio-economic scenario. In the past centuries, there seems to have been an increased involvement of more people thinking about and working to improve the status of women in the world. Governments, non-governmental organizations, funding agencies, small groups and some isolated actions by individuals have been geared towards meeting up with the changes, advancement and development of women. As human societies change overtime with the development of new ways of doing things, women's situations also change. These changes vary from society to society. With the various challenges that globalization has posed, more could be achieved in the shortest possible time if only globalization would work for the benefit of the majority of Indian women in today's global village. Large groups of working women of India are in the rural and unorganized sectors. Socially, the majority of Indian women are still tradition bound and are in a disadvantageous position.

Since globalization is opening up the Indian economy suddenly at a very high speed, without the required economic and social policies to provide the much required safety net, women who have been involved with production in the traditional ways have to cope with numerous problems and yet try to avail of the opportunities which an open economy promises. So, globalization offers many changes and possibilities for women in India, thereby leading to many changes in their life-worlds.

Understanding Cultural Globalization

Cultural globalization refers to "the emergence of a specific set of values and beliefs that are largely shared around the planet"

(Castells, 1997: 117). The source of most global information flows is mass media. Traditionally, this entails a flow of information in a single direction, dispersion from one to many. Throughout the developed world, the globalization of media is often argued to be tantamount to the globalization of culture. Indeed, cultural globalization is familiar to almost everyone; prominent icons of popular culture, such as Coca-Cola and McDonalds are common examples that can be found "everywhere". Looking at global cities (Sassen, 1998) where a consistent brand-name consumerism exists, cultural globalization can appear to act as a solvent, dissolving cultural differences to create homogeneity across the globe.

Women and Cultural Globalization

Major theoretical discourses on globalization have focused on its driving forces as free flow of capital, goods, resources, technology and services due to the new communication and transport technologies. In the search for understanding what cultural and social processes are at work and what implications these may have in our contemporary transnational world, researchers have postulated various hypotheses: about increasing economic integration and a new international division of labour, homogenization (we become more alike) and new patterns of differentiation, time-space compression (Harvey, 1989; Robertson, 1992; Waters, 1995) and time-space distanciation (Giddens, 1990; Inda and Rosaldo, 2002). The latter two concepts especially tell us that the world is shrinking and at the same time stretching out. We may experience the world as smaller than before because it is within reach directly by fast transport and indirectly via new media. Still, the personal world may at the same time be stretching out because social systems are lifted out of the local context, for instance by family members' migration, or through employment by a foreign company.

The forces of globalization, it is argued, work in all directions (north/south, east/west), at all levels (locally and globally) and at a continuously accelerating rate. As a matter of fact, globalization often appears as a ghost feature in literature; as a force that impacts on people's lives all over the globe, but that is identified as little more than a "trend". It tends to appear as an active force, but people are seen as recipients, even victims, of globalization. Women particularly, have been perceived as victims of economic globalization and structural adjustment programmes, leading to a "feminization of the proletariat" (Sassen, 1998). Feminists emphasize new power relations that may affect gender relations and be detrimental to women (Arizpe, 1977; Beneria, 2003; Elson and Pearson, 1997; Fernández-Kelly, 1997). Studies of women's roles in the global economy have centred on the implications of women as a main workforce in export-oriented industry as a consequence of the impact of structural adjustments. Significant contributions have been made in exploring the complicated realities of women's work and lives, revealing the worldwide nature of the "global factory" (Mitter, 1986; Ong, 1987; Visvanathan et al., 1997). While most of the literature has focused on the poor conditions faced by women in free trade zones and multinational firms, one has argued for a contrasting perspective that encompasses the variety of ways in which women strategize economically and socially (Lie and Lund, 1994, 1999). Besides, multinational companies have often provided better salaries and working conditions than the locally-owned businesses or women's uncompensated work in patriarchal households (Lim, 2001). There is great variety not only among the global actors but also in local conditions.

It, therefore, becomes ever more necessary to unravel how globalization processes may lead to new options and even to women's empowerment, as well as to political activism. According to Bhavnani et al. (2003) too, gender identities and gender relations vary across cultures and so do the processes of globalization. Furthermore, not only do globalization processes affect gender relations, but gender as ideology and identity also influences patterns of globalization (Croucher, 2004).

In this context, it becomes imperative to understand the impact of cultural globalization on Indian women. Many sociologists would anticipate that cultural globalization would transform life around the world, and the women are no exception. Appadurai (1996: 52) argued that because of transnational cultural flows associated with migration, tourism and mass media, people now consider "a wider set of possible lives than they ever did before". Because of this, Appadurai (1996: 44) argues that culture has become "less what Pierre Bourdieu would have called a habitus (a tacit realm of reproducible practices and dispositions) and more an arena for conscious choice, justification and representation". According to Pieterse (1994: 149), cultural homogenization is the belief that the so-called global culture follows the global economy and this has led to such phrases as "Cocacolonization" and "McDonaldization". Cultural globalization refers to worldwide cultural standardization – as in "Cocacolonization" and "McDonaldization" – but also to post-colonial culture, cultural pluralism and "hybridization". It is indeed true that the advent of globalization has introduced new cultural celebrations of autonomy and individual choice.

Cultural globalization and accompanying modernity in a globalized and consumer-driven society is the freedom bequeathed to women hitherto bonded by boredom, limitations and silence. Such a freedom however includes the freedom to buy from the marketplace, things to choose, things that define modernity and liberation just as surely as modernity and liberation are the inevitable consequences. New spaces of consumption are structured by constructions of tradition/modernity and public/private in ways that mark them as new, middle-class spaces, gendered in particular ways. While the colonial and earlier nationalist construction of the woman in public was of one who was educated, respectable and modest, spaces of consumption marked by more contemporary forms of globalization portray a more aggressive, confident, sexualized and aggressively public figure. This kind of figure has also had its antecedents, in the figure of the vamp, for example, in popular cinema. However, while the former is sexualized, she is not often understood to be confident, aggressive and titled to her place in the public, which more contemporary, dominant representations of young, globalized Indian femininity reveal. At the same time, globalization of the media and new information technologies is causing the hegemonic spread of consumption patterns that serve the interests of global capital at the expense of sustainable development, and the related growing objectification of women, their bodies and their sexuality.

The various aspects of globalization have promoted growing contacts between different cultures, leading partly to greater understanding and cooperation, and partly to the emergence of transnational communities and hybrid identities. But globalization has also hardened the opposition of different identities. This has taken the form of, inter alia, reactive movements such as fundamentalism, which seek to recuperate traditional patterns, including patriarchal gender relations, in reaction to the "westernizing" trends of globalization. Various forms of identity politics are the paradoxical outgrowth of globalization. The diversity of cultures and sub-cultures is a fact. It does not just signify difference but also variety. The interaction of different cultures may thus be viewed as a positive process, in that it engenders variety which in turn leads to enrichment and expansion: "Cultures enrich one another – this keeps them alive and protects them from museum – like paralysis" (Naumann, 2000: 3).

Possibilities and Opportunities for Women: The Identity Issue

The area of cultural rights is concerned with specific concerns arising in relation to issues of identity and multiculturalism. Debates in this area have direct consequences for women, especially for indigenous women and members of minority communities, who are often faced with a conflict of loyalties between their identity as women and as members of a marginalized community. The social and state responsibility to fight against all traditional and customary practices that discriminate against and harm women, is an essential part of the discussion about cultural rights from a gender perspective. The innate dynamism of modern information technology and of the culture of communication that grows from this technology is likely to end the economic and technological domination embedded in the present form of globalization. One major question which arises here is how are women affecting and have been affected by the wide-ranging advances in information and communication technologies? Is women's agency limited by cultural ceilings in the confines of the masculine order and domesticity? How does one understand the ongoing contradiction of development policy – being efficient and productive as well as pursuing social, gender equality and sustainable human development?

However, on the positive side, globalization has contributed to bring about welcome changes in the lives of women who have been able to avail the opportunities which have opened up in the various sectors of development. With changing attitude towards women, especially in the urban areas, women enjoy more egalitarian set of gender relationship. Positive approach to economic and cultural migration has facilitated women to be exposed to better prospects at the international level. Women in the globalized era are reshuffling between their traditional and modern roles. Within women's group itself, globalization has created the haves and the have-nots, i.e., those who are in an advantageous position due to globalization and those relegated further into disadvantaged position under the new economic policy. Globalization has and continues to have differential impacts on women. But women do not consider their situations to be detrimental to their lives, rather they feel more empowered in comparison to women of previous generations. Walby (2000) argues that to understand the 21st century globalization, the processes of both globalization and modernization need to be considered. These processes have had complex and contradictory effects on women. Modernization has changed gender relations as a result of women's entry into the public sphere. Opening up the economy to global influences has offered some critical challenges to the notions of female dependency. They are in part shaped by the emerging images of the assertive "New Woman". Imbued with agency, she marks the arrival of a gender friendly globalized market (Chakravarti, 2000). Using these new images of independent womanhood, young women construct oppositional narratives of freedom from traditional patriarchal norms and challenge the gender ideologies in their families and society at large. Thus, the traditional domestic roles are challenged in a patriarchal set-up.

In the context of cultural globalization, there is an evidence of increasing contacts between various cultures culminating in greater understanding and formation of transational communities and hybrid identities. Such changes also have considerable impact on the identity formation of women which needs to be effectively addressed. There is no denying the fact that, women have always been discriminated on the basis of caste, class, religion, ethnicity, etc., and when one witnesses the entire process of cultural globalization the situation of women remains all the more problematic. The process of cultural globalization has detrimental effects on the identity of women as reiterated by the exponents of anti-globalization. However, in spite of varied scholarly views on the impact of globalization on women, the chapter tries to explore the issue of identity as a product of globalization.

Globalization, far from destroying it, has been perhaps the most significant force in *creating and proliferating* cultural identity. Manuel Castells devoted an entire volume of his celebrated analysis of "The Information Age" to the proposition that: "Our world and our lives are being shaped by the conflicting trends of globalization and identity". For Castells, the primary *opposition* to the power of globalization lies in "the widespread surge of powerful expressions of collective identity that challenge globalization ... on behalf of cultural singularity and people's control over their lives and environment" (1997: 2). Far from being the fragile flower that globalization tramples, identity is seen here as the upsurging *power* of local culture that offers (albeit multi-form, disorganized and sometimes politically reactionary) *resistance* to the centrifugal force of capitalist globalization. This "power of identity" has given rise to many social movements based around identity positions (gender, sexuality, religion, nationality, etc.). Moreover, as Tomlinson (1999) would remark, identity is not in fact merely some fragile communal-psychic attachment, but a considerable dimension of institutionalized social life in modernity. In modern societies, we live our lives within structures that orchestrate existential experience according to well-policed boundaries. Wé "live" our gender, our sexuality, our nationality and so forth as publicly institutionalized, discursively organized belongings. And in so far as globalization distributes the institutional features of modernity across all cultures, globalization produces "identity" where none existed – where before there were perhaps more particular, more inchoate, less socially policed belongings. In this context, the identity of Indian women was deeply embedded in the patriarchal structures. The power and autonomy exercised by men and their hegemony over women was never to be questioned. Women's inferior position in the patriarchal order and inequality in gender relations were normalized patriarchal structures. But, the "deterritorializing" character of the globalization process has led to the unleashing of cultural forces, thereby leading to the erosion of rigid cultural elements which prohibited gender equality in the patriarchal order. The "hybridization" of identities and penetration of multiculturalism has been powerful enough in challenging the existing patriarchal order in India.

The more obvious examples of this sort of penetration of localities are in such areas of mundane cultural experience as our interaction with globalizing media and communications technologies – television, mobile phones, email, Internet – or in the transformation of local into increasingly "international" food cultures (ibid.). What is at stake in such examples is a transformation in our routine pattern of cultural existence which brings globalized influences, forces, experiences and outlooks into the core of our locally situated life world.

Conclusion

There is no denying the fact that globalization has brought about significant changes in the social life of women. Globalization appears to be a significant force in the psychological development of the people of the 21st century. As a consequence of globalization, the challenges of creating a viable identity are perhaps greater than they have been in the past. According to Giddens (2000: 65), "when globalization alters and erodes traditional ways, identity "has to be created and recreated on a more active basis than before". Identity is less influenced by prescribed social roles and based more on individual choices, on decisions that each person makes about what values to embrace and what paths to pursue in love and work. The area of cultural rights is concerned with specific concerns arising in relation to issues of identity and multiculturalism. Many women who are now awakening to this crucial period of human evolution are carrying within them the seeds of global transformation.

Women of every generation, race, nationality and ability are poised in potential, waiting for an inner cue to begin a peaceful revolution, to answer the impelling call of evolution. Modern women, utilizing the feminine skills of inclusive nurturing, team work, intuition, compromise and attention to the long view are now stepping into every field, and personally model a new approach in every field of endeavour. The global feminism culture provides a frame to reconcile to some extent differences and to find grounds of common interest to promote women welfare all over the world. Intercultural dialogue is an effective means to overcome cultural crises, but it remains one of the crucial challenges facing the 21st century generations.

References

Albrow, M. *The Global Age*. Cambridge: Polity Press, 1996.

Appadurai, A. *Modernity at Large: Cultural Dimensions of Globalisation*. Minneapolis, MN: University of Minnesota, 1996.

Arizpe, Lourdes. "Women in the Informal Sector: The Case of Mexico City", *Signs* 3, Autumn 1977: 25–37.

Barth, Fredrik. "Scale and Network in Urban Western Society", in *Scale and Social Organization*, ed. F. Barth, Oslo: Scandinavian University Press, 1978, 163–83.

Bauman, Zygmunt. *Globalisation: The Human Consequences*. Cambridge: Polity Press, 1998.

Beneria, L. *Gender, Development and Globalisation: Economics as if People Mattered*. New York: Routledge, 2003.

Bhavnani, K.K. et al., eds. *Feminist Futures: Re-imagining Women, Culture and Development*. London: Zed Books, 2003.

Castells, M. *The Power of Identity*, Vol. II of *The Information Age: Economy, Society and Culture*. Oxford: Blackwell, 1997.

Chakravarti, U. "State, Market and Freedom of Expression: Women and the Electronic Media", Special Issue, *Economic and Political Weekly (Review of Women's Studies)*, April 2000, 12–17.

Croucher, S.L. *Globalization and Belonging: The Politics of Identity in a Changing World*. Maryland: Rowman and Littlefield Publishers, 2004.

Elson, E. and R. Pearson. 1997. "The Subordination of Women and the Internationalization of Factory Production", in *Women and Irish Society: A Sociological Reader*, eds. N. Visvanathan, L. Duggan, L. and N. Wiegersma, Belfast: Beyond the Pale.

Fernández-Kelly, M.P. "Maquiladoras: The Vision from the Inside", in *The Women, Gender and Development Reader*, eds. N. Visvanathan et al., London: Zed Books, 1997, 203–15.

Giddens, A. *The Consequences of Modernity*. Cambridge: Polity Press, 1990.

——. *Runaway World: How Globalisation is Reshaping Our Lives*. New York: Routledge, 2000.

Harvey, D. *The Condition of Post-modernity: An Enquiry into the Origins of Cultural Change*. Oxford: Blackwell, 1989.

Inda, J.X. and R. Rosaldo, eds. *The Anthropology of Globalization: A Reader*. Oxford: Blackwell, 2002.

Lie, M. and R. Lund. *Renegotiating Local Values*. London: NIAS/Curzon, 1994.

——. "Globalisation, Place and Gender", *AI & Society* 13 (1–2), 1999: 107–23.

Lim, L.Y.C. "Capitalism, Imperialism and Patriarchy: The Dilemma of Third World Women Workers in Multinational Factories", in *Development Sociology: Actor Perspectives*, ed. N. Long, London: Routledge, 2001.

Mitter, S. *Common Fate, Common Bond: Women in the Global Economy*. London: Pluto Press, 1986.

Nash, J. and M.P. Fernandez-Kelly. *Women, Men and the International Division of Labour*. Albany: State University of New York Press, 1983.

Naumann, M. *A Dialogue of Cultures*, in Deutschland; 3/2000, (June/July), E7; Frankfurt am Main: 3, 2000.

Ong, A. *Spirits of Resistance and Capitalist Discipline: Factory Workers in Malaysia*. Albany, NY: SUNY Press, 1987.

Pieterse, J.N. "Unpacking the West: How European is Europe?", in *Racism, Modernity and Identity*, eds. A. Rattansi and S. Westwood, Cambridge: Polity Press, 1994, 129–49.

Robertson, R. *Globalization: Social Theory and Global Culture*. London: Sage, 1992.

Sen, A. Foreword, Make Trade Fair, Oxfam 2002, http://www.maketradefair.com/

Sassen, S. *Globalization and its Discontents*. New York: The New Press, 1998.

——. "Women's Burden: Counter-Geographies of Globalization and the Feminization of Survival", *Journal of International Affairs* 53 (2), 2000: 503–25.

Symington, A. "Re-Inventing Globalization for Women's Rights and Development", in *Re-Inventing Globalization: Highlights of AWID'S 9th International Forum on Women's Rights in Development*, Guadalajara, Mexico, AWID Canada, 3–6 October 2002.

Tomlinson, J. *Globalization and Culture*. Cambridge: Polity Press, 1999.

Visvanathan, N. et al., eds. *The Women, Gender and Development Reader*. London: Zed Books, 1997.

Walby, S. "Analyzing Social Inequality in the Twenty-First Century: Globalization and Modernity Restructure Inequality", *Contemporary Sociology* 28 (8), 2000: 13–18.

Waters, Malcolm. *Globalization*. London: Routledge, 1995.

7

Globalization and Social Exclusion

The Social Location of Scheduled Castes in Indian Society and the Need for Inclusion

Indu Upadhyay

After the adoption of economic reforms in 1991, it was expected that the socio-economic conditions of the weaker sections would improve since it would bring about more opportunities for every section of the society. It should however be pointed out that the conditions of the weaker sections have become more deplorable. Therefore, the present chapter is an attempt to study the socio-economic conditions of the Dalits. "Dalit" means a person who is oppressed or downtrodden. Here, Dalit stands for Scheduled Castes (SCs). The indicators selected for the purpose are literacy, employment and poverty. The study attempts to bring about a comparative analysis of the socio-economic conditions of the SCs and the general category population after adoption of the economic reforms in 1991.

The objective of the study is to study the impact of globalization on the Indian economy; to comparatively analyse the impact of globalization on the SCs and others, to suggest various measures for the upliftment of the SCs.

The study is based on secondary source of information. Secondary data were collected from various reports such as material published by RBI such as Reserve Bank of India Bulletin, Currency and Finance Reports, and various reports of Planning Commission such as reports of various five-year plans. The study is divided into three sections. While the first section is an introduction, the second section throws light on the impact of globalization on SCs, and the third section focuses on the conclusions and the findings of the study.

I
Introduction

The international capitalist economy is undergoing a process of fundamental transformation in the organizations of production accompanied by institutional arrangements necessary for such transformation. Neo-liberalism, the structural adjustment policy of the World Bank and the International Monetary Fund, and the WTO followed by the new GATT agreement constitute the institutional framework for transnational capitalism. This transformation since the last two decades is known as the process of globalization.Two more processes, namely, privatization and liberalization accompany it. In fact, the phenomenon of globalization is not new to the world because the historical processes of wealth and poverty creation are interconnected. From ancient days, trade and transport have brought the world together. Earlier there were attempts such as Napoleonic wars, industrial revolution, Russian revolution, etc. However, their impact remained limited. The present process of globalization is qualitatively and radically different from the earlier ones. Since 1970s, it has brought a radical restructuring of the world economy. Now, there is a new political economy in the process of making which is information driven. Capitalism and IT are the driving forces. It is holistic, multidimensional and therefore truly global in nature.

Globalization is making a considerable impact on all the aspects of human life in all the countries in the world. It is imperative to understand this process and study the nature of the impact on various communities. It is making its impact even on the developed countries. The impact is social, economic, political, cultural and even moral in nature. Since globalization is truly universal in nature, it naturally involves competition and quality. No individual would escape from these. And there is no point in avoiding these. Quality and competition are the watchwords in the age of globalization. Fortunately, the Indian society has all the potentialities of these two. Moreover, unlike the United Nations, the WTO expects the members to accept at present any one service to be thrown open to all the members in the world. Therefore, there is no alternative to competition. And without quality, competition would have no meaning. Here, the other processes of liberalization and privatization are going to play an important role. Therefore, it is necessary to bring about changes to cope up with the changes. India is a plural society having many sections based on religion, caste, class, etc. These sections have different types of impacts at different levels. It will be academically unfair to think about the impact of globalization unilaterally. Different sections or groups in a heterogeneous society have different problems. Even after 60 years of independence, various social groups are not empowered to face the challenge of competing equality. Even now, they need the positive support of the welfare state. In view of this, what is necessary is to have a rational balance between empowerment of weaker sections and the achievement of quality to face the competition.

It needs no emphasis that a few societies have condemned one of their sections to physical segregation as the Hindu society has done in the case of the former untouchables. The mere physical touch of an untouchable was a sin, an abomination. The segregation of a section of the Hindus as untouchables, precluded from such elementary rights as entry to public temples or the use of public wells and tanks, and whose physical touch contaminated a member of the higher castes, constituted a most inhuman form of social oppression. The untouchables were the outcastes of the

Hindu society. Hallowed with tradition and sanctified by religion, the unsociability continued to exist in all its barbarous vigour for centuries.

After independence, in 1950, the Constitution of India abolished untouchability (Article 17) and in 1955, the Parliament passed the Untouchability Offences Act. The national movement had created an atmosphere sympathetic towards the untouchables. It made it possible for the government to provide protective discrimination in an attempt to pull out the untouchables from traditional segregation. Among the multitude of difficult tasks facing the new nation of India in 1947, none was more challenging than the integration of the most deprived 15 per cent of its population – the untouchables – into unequal partnership in the emerging modern republic.

Since the Government of India Act 1935, the untouchables became known as the SCs. But even though untouchability and discrimination on the basis of caste are constitutionally outlawed and despite the constitutional legal support and also efforts by various voluntary agencies, it is commonly observed that they continue to be deprived of their rightful place in the society. And upper castes have generally denied equal treatment to the SCs.

The backwardness of the SCs will be evident from their unemployment, dependence on agriculture, illiteracy and social segregation. In terms of residence, housing and health conditions, the condition of the SCs is precarious. Even now in many villages they have to suffer residential segregation and direct and indirect social boycott. There are many among them who are too poor to build their houses. On account of their poverty and unhygienic living conditions, they, in large numbers, suffer from malnutrition, physical disabilities and diseases such as tuberculosis, leprosy, malaria and other general diseases.

This is not to say that the post-independence period has not brought any socio-economic and political changes in the lives of the SCs. Constitutional provisions, political process since independence and the impact of leadership of Dr B.R. Ambedkar have created a wave of rising expectations in the lives of SCs in general and in the lives of the neo-Buddhists in particular. Gradually, since then, the SCs are slowly becoming aware of their rightful place in the society and are asserting for reordering of the society for their betterment and advancement. This has created a number of pressures and pulls resulting in socio-political tensions in the Indian society.

Present Scenario

There are a good number of studies on the neo-Buddhists, the dominant SCs in Maharashtra. However, there are very few studies on other SCs such as *Mang, Chamar, Dhor, Mochi, Bhangi,* etc. Moreover, most of the studies are based on single or two variables such as caste or/and class. It is to be remembered that in a complex society such as India, single-factor analysis gives a one-sided picture, which is far away from the philosophy of globalization. It is therefore necessary to study the nature and impact of the SCs movement, impact of government policies, also the impact of the efforts of the voluntary agencies and most importantly the impact of the political processes during last 60 years. Owing to the democratic process since independence, increasing means of communication and the spread of education, there is increasing awareness among all the sections of society and the SCs are no exceptions to it. The Constitution has released the forces of liberalism. Because of these forces, an era of politicization has started in all walks of life and the traditional gap between politics and society has come to an end. Now politics has become a new instrument for achieving socio-economic development. Socio-economic development of the SCs would be the precondition for their integration in the mainstream of the society, which the constitution has visualized. Much has been done by way of constitutional provisions, administrative efforts and proper response from a larger section of the upper castes. However, whatever is done is not enough to match the rising expectations of the weaker sections including the SCs. Still they are unorganized and constitute the larger deprived sections of the population. On the other hand, the organized sections even in SCs have grabbed the benefits of socio-economic development. If we want to analyse this reality, the study should be interdisciplinary and based on variables – caste, class, religion, region, ideology, gender, identity, etc. Because the problem of the SCs is interdisciplinary, having many dimensions, and complex, it is also dynamic in nature.

We have accepted a democratic form of government in an undemocratic society. It is, therefore, necessary to give political education to the people about the need and genesis of welfare policies for the weaker sections. Political education means education about nature, working and the functions of a political system in which you live. This was the duty of the elites and the leaders in the political process. Unfortunately, both have miserably failed in their tasks. As a result of it, there is a lack of understanding about the problems of the weaker sections which results in social tensions.

There is a lack of political will regarding the development of SCs. There is increasing populism to fetch the votes of SCs and very few sincere efforts for their development. Many a times, the political process divides the SCs. It is observed that the welfare schemes remain on paper, but because of the policies there is a backlash among the upper castes.

In Maharashtra it was experienced that 20 per cent budgetary provision in Panchayati Raj bodies is not spent and the amount is transferred to the main budget to other items. There are five development corporations for the welfare of the SCs and the Other Backward Classes (OBCs), but for a long time their evaluation has not been made. The amounts declared, amounts sanctioned and the actual amounts spent are different. The last one being very meager (Karade, 2008).

Three points emerge from such a situation. Firstly, the policy provisions by the political process create unrest among the upper castes, as there is no adequate political education. Secondly, despite constitutional and legal provisions, the SCs still remain deprived of their adequate due in the nation's development. And lastly, the injustice on the part of the SCs still continues in different forms, which lead to increasing social tensions and social disintegration.

Challenges of Globalization

In fact, it is high time that the leaders in the political process and academicians give a serious thought to the consequences of liberalization, privatization and particularly globalization.

In globalization, the old concepts such as nationalism, sovereignty are gradually waning and then there is an erosion of a nation-state. Samuel Huntington (1993) argues that now the culture would be an important variable in international politics and not concepts such as nationalism or sovereignty. There is increasing international interdependence on the one hand giving rise to internationalism. On the other hand, the narrow and parochial loyalties are playing significant role. How to reconcile this contradiction? Here, we need long-term as well as short-term policies and avoid aphorism, opportunism and populism. As we have seen above, globalization needs quality and the quality assumes acquiring various skills necessary for individual and social development. Because of the changing nature of economy and social conditions, now there are new needs which have arisen in society, now new sections have come up in the society and they have non-traditional needs. They include the needs of senior citizens, the employed married couples in metropolitan cities and the demand for crèche is on increase. Multiplexes, food malls, shopping malls, etc., have changed the lifestyle of the middle class. In this way, new needs can be found out and an attempt can be made to give response to these demands by way of providing service to them. The 21st century is a century of multi-skills and a person having more than one skill will definitely have a bright future.

Dr Ambedkar gave a message – "educates, agitates and organizes" (dalitandrtribe.wordpress.com). But what kind of education? The present education is fast becoming irrelevant to the changing needs. It is to be understood that the present education system is the product of the colonial rule and the post-independence period and the governments have done very little to change the same. In addition to increasing educational opportunities, our demand should be to make the education system more meaningful and more relevant to the changing needs in the society. It may be remembered in a way that the present unemployment is mostly false one. It is unemployment of the unskilled people (Joshi and Little, 1996). Therefore, an attempt is to be made to improve the quality of the people. It can be achieved by way of acquiring knowledge, skills and attitudes in the changing context. Globalization has posed a challenge to all and more to the SCs. Unless such efforts are done, the values in the constitution would not be materialized. Therefore, the present chapter is an attempt to study the socio-economic position of the SCs in India, draw conclusion from the study and suggest various measures for the upliftment of the SCs.

II
Conceptual Framework

Inclusive growth demands that all social groups should have equal access to services provided by the state and equal opportunity for upwards economic and social mobility. It is also necessary to ensure that there is no discrimination against any section of our society. In India, certain groups such as SCs, STs, OBCs and minorities have historically been disadvantaged and vulnerable. Our Constitution contains various provisions for the development of such marginalized sections, for instance, Article 341 for SCs, Article 342 for STs, Article 340 for OBCs, Article 30 which provides the right to minorities to establish educational institutions and so on. Their individual and social growth however cannot be ensured without improving their surroundings and providing clean drinking water, toilets and educational opportunities.

The present chapter deals with the efforts made for socio-economic development of SCs. The indicators selected for purpose are education, employment opportunities, availability of basic amenities, access to income earning assets, poverty and Human Development Index (HDI).

Socio-economic Conditions of Scheduled Castes

The SCs constitute 16.23 per cent of India's population. In the past, they have been socially and economically exploited and denied human dignity and the sense of self-worth.[1] It needs no emphasis that people belonging to SC community are spread all over the country, with 80 per cent of them living in rural areas. They constitute more than a fifth of the population of Uttar Pradesh, Punjab, Himachal Pradesh and West Bengal. More than half of the SCs population is concentrated in the five states of Uttar Pradesh (35.1 million), West Bengal (18.4 million), Tamil Nadu (11.8 million), Andhra Pradesh (12.3 million) and Bihar (13 million). In spite of giving a positive discrimination for their development, the SCs face various atrocities in the Indian society.

Table 7.1
Comparative Incident of Crime Against SCs

Crime Head	*Year*					*% Variation in 2005 over 2004*
	2001	*2002*	*2003*	*2004*	*2005*	
Murder	763	739	581	654	669	2.3
Rape	1,316	1,331	1,089	1,157	1,172	1.3
Kidnapping and Abduction	400	319	232	253	258	2.0
Dacoity	41	29	24	26	26	0.0
Robbery	133	105	70	72	80	11.1
Hurt	4,547	4,491	3,969	3,824	3,847	0.6
Protection of Civil Right Act	633	1018	634	364	291	–20.20
SC/ST(Prevention of Atrocities) Act	13,113	10,770	8,048	8,891	8497	–4.4
Arson	354	322	204	211	210	–0.5
Others	12,201	14,383	11,401	11,435	11,077	–3.1
Total	33,501	33,507	26,252	26,887	26,127	–2.8

Source: Crime in India-2005, National Crime Records Bureau, Ministry of Home Affairs.

Table 7.1 shows that 654 SCs were murdered in 2004 which increased by 2.3 per cent in 2005 to 669. Also, 1,157 rapes were done against them in 2004, which increased to 1,172 in 2005, and 253 kidnappings and abductions were done against them which increased to 2.0 per cent within one year. Two important protective legislations are in operation for people belonging to the SC community, the Protection of Civil Rights Act, 1955 and the Scheduled Castes and Scheduled Tribes (Prevention of Atrocities) Act, 1989. However, despite these constitutional provisions, atrocities and crimes on members of SCs, especially women, continue to occur in all parts of the country in varying degrees. As per the National Crime Records Bureau Report 2005, the crimes against SCs in the last few years were mainly atrocities followed by hurt and rape. Data for the last five years are reproduced in Table 7.1.

Table 7.2

Population and Decadal Growth Rate of SCs and STs (1971–2001)

Year	*Population*		*Decadal Growth Rate*	
	Total	*SC*	*Total*	*SC*
1971	548.1	80.0	24.8	24.2
1981	683.4	104.7	24.7	30.7
1991	846.3	138.2	23.8	32.0
2001	1028.6	166.6	21.5	20.5

Source: Sub Plan, Guidelines for Implementation, Planning Commission, New Delhi, 2006, p. 3.

The forces of urbanization, social and protective legislations, positive discrimination and other measures taken by the government, have led to a gradual improvement in occupational mobility and living standards over the years, but the living conditions of the majority of SCs continue to show socio-economic backwardness. The SC population in the country in 1971 was 80 million which has increased to 166.6 million in 2001. The SC population had a decadal growth rate of 20.5 per cent during 1991 and 2001 as in the case of general population, though it had experienced higher growth rates of 21.5 per cent during 1981 and 1991.

Table 7.3

Sex Ratio: SC and Total Population

Year	*SC*	*Total Population*
1971	935	930
1981	932	934
1991	922	927
2001	936	933

Source: Sub Plan, Guidelines for Implementation, Planning Commission, New Delhi, 2006, p. 3.

As can be seen from the Table 7.3, the sex ratio (females per 1,000 males) for SCs has declined over the last 30 years. The declining sex ratio of SCs could be attributed to higher female mortality and their limited access to health services. Such developments are surely a matter of concern for gender equality within the disadvantaged group. Sex ratio for SCs was 935 in 1971 which was 930 for the total population. It increased to 936 in 2001 for SCs and 933 for total population. No doubt, the sex ratio has improved for both the categories still there is a scope for betterment because even now there are 933 females after every 1,000 males, this is a kind of discrimination against the female child which needs to be corrected by the society.

Table 7.4

Literacy Rate of General Population and SC Population (1961–2001)

Year	*General*			*SC*		
	Male	*Female*	*Total*	*Male*	*Female*	*Total*
1961	33.44	12.95	24.02	16.96	3.29	10.27
1971	39.45	18.70	29.45	22.36	6.44	14.67
1981	46.89	24.82	36.23	31.12	10.93	21.38
1991	64.1	39.3	52.2	49.91	23.76	37.41
2001	75.3	53.7	64.8	66.64	41.90	54.69

Source: Census of India.

It should however be pointed out that status of the SCs can be understood by the spread of education among the population belonging to the SC category. Education provides oneself with an opportunity to cope up with the situation which is changing day by day by providing skills of various kinds to any section of the community.

Although the literacy rate of SCs has increased considerably as can be seen from the Table 7.4. The literacy rate of SCs was 10.27 per cent in 1961 which increased to 14.67 per cent in 1971. In the year 1981, it was 21.38 per cent which increased to 37.41 per cent in 1991. Further, in 2001, it increased to 54.69 per cent. However, the gap between the literacy rate of people belonging to general category and those of SC which was there in 1961 still persists in 2001. The literacy rate of population belonging to general category was 64.8 per cent in 2001, while it was only 54.69 per cent for SCs. However, literacy among the SCs female is quite low, i.e., 41.90 per cent against 53.70 per cent of general female, which is a cause of great concern. Growth rate of literacy among SC females between the two decennial Census 1991 and 2001 is 18 per cent points. However, 456 districts out of total of 582 districts inhabited by SCs, the literacy among SCs is less than average literacy rate of non-SC/ST population. The literacy rate among the SCs continues to be much lower than the all-India level for the states: Bihar (28.5%), Rajasthan (52.2%), Madhya Pradesh (58.6%), Uttar Pradesh (46.3%) and Andhra Pradesh (53.5%) (Sub Plan, Guidelines for Implementation, Planning Commission, New Delhi, 2006, p. 3).

Table 7.5

Gross Enrolment Ratios (2003–04)

Category	*I–V*	*I–VIII*
General	98.2	84.8
SC	92.97	69.63

Source: Sub Plan, Guidelines for Implementation, Planning Commission, New Delhi, 2006, p. 4.

Table 7.5 shows that the enrolment ratio in Classes I–VIII indicates 84.8 per cent for general population and 69.63 per cent for SCs. Primary education up to the level of V, which is essential for all-round development of any category of the society, even after passing of 20 years of structural reforms, still near about 8 per cent of the SCs do not avail the benefits of primary education up to the level of V. In the area of higher education also, there is a gap between the SCs and the general population. The gross enrolment ratio for the whole country as a whole in 2000 was about 10 per cent for the SCs, however it was significantly lower at 6.4 per cent.

The school dropout rate is a crucial indicator of lack of educational development. The dropout rate for SC children is very high. In Classes I to V it is 32.7 per cent, 55.2 per cent in Classes I to VIII and 69.1 per cent in Classes I to X in 2004–05 as is evident from the Table 7.6. While in the same year, the dropout rate of general children was: I–V – 31.47 per cent, I–VIII – 52.32 per cent, I–X – 62.69 per cent. The cause behind this may be that most of the SC parents are poverty ridden, so they are not in a position to send their children to school, in spite of the fact that they are provided free fooding and clothing facilities at the school. It needs no emphasis that social discrimination does not seems to be the cause behind the rising dropout rate since there is a little difference between the dropout rate of the general children and the children belonging to the category of SC. It should however be pointed that in spite of giving a positive discrimination in favour of Dalits, the dropout rate of the children is approximately 70 per cent that means that the children are not interested in studies; therefore an improvement is required in the quality of education at the primary level. Dropout among the SCs is much higher in Classes I–VIII and I–X (55.2% and 69.1%, respectively) as against the general population (52.32% and 62.69%, respectively). The dropout rate is much higher among the SC girl students, which is a cause of concern. One of the cause behind this may be the household duties which the girls are expected to do and other cause can be the secondary status given to a girl in any family be it SC family or general family.

Table 7.6

Dropout Rates, 2004–05 – SCs (Provisional)

Category	*Classes I–V*			*Classes I–VIII*			*Classes I–X*		
	All	*Boys*	*Girls*	*All*	*Boys*	*Girls*	*All*	*Boys*	*Girls*
General	31.47	33.79	28.57	52.32	51.85	52.92	62.69	60.98	64.92
SC	32.7	36.1	34.2	55.2	60.0	57.3	69.1	74.2	71.3

Source: Selected Educational Statistics 2004–05, Ministry of Human Resource Development.

It should however be pointed out that reservation in the educational institutions and financial assistance constitute perhaps the most important factor in the educational development of Dalits. It is primarily responsible to make the basic input of education available and affordable to them. The reforms have already resulted in freezing the grants to many institutions and in stagnating if not lowering the expenditure on education[2]. It needs no emphasis that product prices are not only based on the demand-supply consideration in their market segment but also on promotional strategies. In a true spirit of globalization, many foreign universities are invading the educational spheres which are beyond the reach of the Dalits. Even in the sphere of primary education the coverage of which has been so miserably inadequate that it leaves multitude of children in villages as illiterate.

Next indicator which shows the development of Harijans is employment facility. Employment is the opportunity to a person which leads not only to the satisfaction of basic requirements, but also to the betterment of the standard of living of the concerned person. In 2000, the CDS employment rate in rural areas was 46 per cent for SC male workers, compared with 48.40 per cent for other male workers. Similarly, the CDS employment rate for SC workers in urban area was 45.8 per cent compared to 49.9 per cent for other households. Disparities between the SCs and others are also reflected in the unemployment rate. Unemployment rate based on CDS for SCs was about 5 per cent as compared to about 3.5 per cent for other workers in rural and urban areas. The NSSO data on wage earning revealed disparities in labour wages for SCs and others. For instance, in 1999–2000, the average weekly wage earning of an SC worker (at 1993–94 price) was ₹ 174.50 compared to ₹ 197.05 for other workers (Dubey, 2003).

Available empirical evidence suggests discrimination against SCs in employment, wages, credit and so on. These factors have acted as constraints to their occupational mobility. In urban areas, too, there is prevalence of discrimination by caste; particularly discrimination in employment, which operates at least in part through traditional mechanisms; SCs are disproportionately represented in poorly paid, dead-end jobs. Further, there is a flawed, preconceived notion that they lack merit and are unsuitable for formal employment.

As can be seen from Table 7.7, 40.41 per cent of the total population of SCs are workers, of which 45.61 per cent are agricultural labourers as compared to 26.55 per cent at all-India level. The position is reversed when we come to the share of SCs among cultivator, which is 19.99 per cent as compared to 31.65 per cent for all workers. That means only 19.99 per cent of the total SC population is involved in decision-making in the agricultural sector. It needs no emphasis that only 3.99 per cent of SCs are workers to household industrial sector, the reason behind this is that they lack skills necessary for employment in the industrial sector.

Table 7.8 shows the representation of SCs in the Central Government services. It shows marginal improvement of the overall SC representation in Group A, B and C categories of Central Government from 1994 to 2004. Representation of SCs in Group A services increased from 10.25 per cent to 12.2 per cent, in case of Group B services it stood at 12.06 per cent in 1994 which increased to 14.5 per cent; further in Group C services SCs representation increased from 15.73 per cent in 1994 to 16.9 per cent in 2001. On the other hand, their was substantial decline in Group D category from 20.47 per cent to 18.4 per cent during the same period. The point to be noted here is that even in 2004, the representation of SC population in Central Government services was

Table 7.7

Percentage of Working and Non-Working Population (Total and SCs, 2001)

	Total Workers		*Cultivators*		*Agricultural*		*Household Industry*		*Other Worker*		*Non-Worker*	
	All	*SC*	*All*	*SC*	*All*	*SC*	*All*	*SC*	*All*	*SC*	*All*	*SC*
India	39.10	40.41	31.65	19.99	26.55	45.61	4.22	3.99	37.59	30.49	60.20	59.00
Rural	41.75	42.50	40.24	23.47	33.05	52.23	3.72	3.73	22.80	20.58	58.25	57.50
Urban	32.75	33.14	2.31	1.76	4.71	11.03	5.22	4.84	87.27	82.37	67.75	67.86

Note: All include (SCs).

Source: Census 2001.

Table 7.8

SC Representations in Central Government Services

Group	*1994*			*1999*			*2004*		
	Total	*SC*	*% Total*	*Total*	*SC*	*% Total*	*Total*	*SC*	*% Total*
A	59,016	6,046	10.25	93,520	10,558	11.29	80,011	9,744	12.2
B	10,318	12,442	12.06	1,04,963	13,306	12.68	1,35,409	19,802	14.5
C	2,381,613	3,74,758	15.73	2,396,426	3,78,115	15.78	2,040,970	3,44,865	16.9
D	1,023,285	2,09,423	20.47	9,49,353	1,89,761	19.99	8,02,116	1,47,212	18.4
Total	3,567,112	6,02,670	16.9	3,54,262	5,91,740	16.7	3,058,506	5,21,423	17.9

Source: Report of Eleventh Plan, GoI.

only 17.5 per cent, while 82.95 per cent was occupied by the general category people.

Another important dimension of discrimination is the wide gap between SCs and rest of the population with respect to the basic amenities such as electricity, banking services, *pucca* houses, water supply, toilet facilities, drainage and telephone facilities.

In 2000, about two-thirds of rural SC households were landless and less than one-third of the SC household had acquired access to capital assets, compared to 60 per cent among the others. Similar disparity exists in the status of health of SCs. The incidence of anaemia among women and mortality rate among children are higher than other groups.[3] The cumulative impact of all these disparities therefore is reflected in the high levels of poverty, about 36 per cent among SCs as compared to only 21 per cent among others.

Table 7.9

Population Below Poverty Line – SCs (in %)

Category	*1993–94*		*2004–05*		*Percentage Decrease*	
	Rural	*Urban*	*Rural*	*Urban*	*Rural*	*Urban*
All*	37.30	32.40	28.30	25.70	(–) 9.00	(–) 6.70
SC	48.11	49.48	36.80	39.90	(–) 11.31	(–) 9.58
Gap	10.81	17.08	8.0	14.20	(–) 2.31	(–) 2.78

*Includes SC population.

Source: Perspective Planning Division, Planning Commission, New Delhi.

Due to lack of access of fixed sources of income and high incidence of wage labour associated with high rate of under-employment and low wages, SC households are often faced with low income and high incidence of poverty which is shown in Table 7.9. In 2004–05, about 36.80 per cent of SC people were BPL in rural areas as compared to only 28.30 per cent for others. In urban areas, the gap was slightly larger, 39.90 per cent of SC households were BPL compared to 25.70 per cent among other households.

Human Development Index (HDI) and Human Poverty Index (HPI): According to the UNDP India Report (2007) on Human Poverty and Socially Disadvantaged Groups in India, the HDI at all-India level is estimated to be 0.303 which is lower than the HDI for non-SC/ST at 0.393 for the period 1980–2000. The variation across states is very large, ranging from 0.61 for Kerala to 0.195 for Bihar.[4]

The HPI is a measure to assess the level of deprivation among a given social group with reference to infant mortality rate, illiteracy rate, poverty ratio, health status and national status. The value of HPI was estimated at 33.63 per cent for all the social groups taken together. The HPI for SCs was estimated to be 41.47 per cent at all-India level. The HPI revealed significant variation across the states with values ranging from 18.62 to 59.36 per cent. The level of deprivation was greatest in Bihar (59.36%), followed by Uttar Pradesh (50.03%), Orissa (47.66%), Rajasthan (43.78%) and Madhya Pradesh (43.68%) as compared to all-India level of 41.47 per cent. In the remaining 11 states, the rate of deprivation was lower than all-India value. Deprivation was 18.62 per cent in Kerala, which was found to be least.[5] Along with the general population, the percentage of both SCs living below the poverty line has indicated a declining trend from 1993–94 to 2004–05. The need for special attention for SCs' welfare and development was realized when it was found that the SCs suffer from the dual disabilities of severe economic exploitation and social discrimination. While they constitute 16.2 per cent of the total population of the country, their proportion is much larger – more than twice in the poverty groups of the country, most of the SCs are below the poverty line. Accordingly, thrust has to be on the economic development of the SCs. In respect of the SCs, the strategy is to take up programmes for the SCs in different occupational categories, especially the poverty groups. The SCs are mostly landless labourers, marginal and small farmers, leather workers, fishermen, artisans such as weavers and those who follow strenuous occupations such as rickshaw pullers, cart pullers, etc. The approach is to reach the flow of benefits to the SCs through individual family and group-oriented programmes. For this, new need-based programmes are required to be taken up and the existing programmes re-oriented to suit the specific developmental requirements and handicaps of the SCs in different occupational groups.

Table 7.10

Status of Key Health Indicators

Category	*SC*	*General*
Infant Mortality	83.0	67.6
Neo-Natal Mortality	53.2	43.4
Child Mortality	39.5	29.3
Under-Five Mortality	119.3	94.9
ANC Check Up	61.1	65.4
% of Institutional Deliveries	26.8	33.6
% of Women with Anaemia	56.0	51.8
% of Children Under-nourished (Weight for Age)	53.5	47.0
Childhood Vaccination (Full Immunization)	40.2	42.0

Source: Sub Plan, Guidelines for Implementation, Planning Commission, New Delhi, 2006, p. 4.

Table 7.10 shows that most of the key health indicators indicate a gap of 5–10-point difference between SCs and general population. Infant mortality rate (IMR) is 83 for SCs and 67.6 for the general population. Child mortality is also quite high among the SCs which is 39.5 in comparison to 29.3 for the general population. Even after so many years of adoption of globalization, still more than 70 per cent of the deliveries are done at home under the supervision of untrained village quacks which leads to an ever-increasing maternal mortality rate of women belonging to SC community. Since they belong to BPL group, therefore they are not in the position to consume nutritious food so they suffer from anaemia. About 53.5 per cent of the children belonging to SC category are under-nourished because they have lower weight than normal children. About 40.2 per cent children are immunized, while about 60 per cent SC children are exposed to health risks due to the ignorance of the parents or their poor economic conditions. Since SCs belong to BPL category, therefore they are unable to provide their children with a nutritious diet, which leads to poor health conditions of the children. More than half of the children are not immunized not because their parents cannot afford to do this (immunization is provided free of cost in villages to the family belonging to BPL), but due to the religious dogmas and superstitions.

Table 7.11

Electricity Facility (as per Census 2001)

Census Year	*Per cent of Household Having Access to Electricity*		
	Total	*General*	*SC*
1991	42.4	48.1	28.1
2001	55.8	61.4	44.4

Source: Sub Plan, Guidelines for Implementation, Planning Commission, New Delhi, 2006, p. 4.

The Table 7.11 indicates that only 28.1 per cent SC households had access to electricity in comparison to the general population (48.1%) in 1991. The condition has slightly improved in 2001 indicating that 44.4 per cent SCs households have access to electricity in comparison to 61.4 per cent of the general population. No doubt, the condition has improved but still near about 60 per cent of the SC population is not getting access to electricity. The point to be noted is that though access to electricity is not included as an indicator of poverty line, but electricity plays an important role in life of every person, therefore one can say that even after connection of the whole world still inequality persists in India.

Table 7.12

Percentage of People Having Safe Drinking Water Facility

Total Households Having Drinking Water Source by Location					*General and SC Households Having Water Source by Location*			
Total Number of Households	*Percentage*				*Total Number of Households*	*Percentage*		
	Within Premises	*Near Premises*	*Away*			*Within Premises*	*Near Premises*	*Away*
53,692,376	65.4	25.2	9.4	General	43,555,288	69.4	22.6	8
				SC	7,808,556	48.5	36.8	14.7

Source: Sub Plan, Guidelines for Implementation, Planning Commission, New Delhi, 2006, p. 4.

Position of improved drinking water facility in SC households also indicates improvement during the decade 1991–2001 as is evident from Table 7.12. But there is a need to further improve the facilities of drinking-water supply to all. Still less than half of the SCs have access to clean drinking water at their residence, 36.8 per cent take water near premises and 14.7 per cent have to travel away to get clean drinking water.

III
Conclusions

There is no denying of the fact that 80 per cent of the SCs still live in rural areas and economic exploitation remains their most acute problem. They are overwhelmingly marginal farmers or landless labourers. Large numbers migrate to cities or labour-scarce rural areas such as Punjab. Many are in debt and are obliged to work off their debts through debt-bonded labour despite the fact that this practice was abolished by law in 1976. In these cases, a labourer takes a loan from a landlord or moneylender and in return agrees to work for that person until the debt is repaid. In practice, it is difficult to repay the debt as interest payments are high and cumulative, and poverty forces the labourer deeper into debt. The debt can be passed onto the next generation and thus it is impossible to escape the cycle. In some areas, many high-caste landlords pay their SC labourers minimum wages in cash or food, or nothing at all, and any resistance is frequently met by violence, sometimes resulting in the death or injury of the victim. Sexual harassment against SC women is frequent. Mob violence against SC communities is frequently reported, sometimes led by landlords or community leaders, and has been especially noticeable in situations where SC workers have joined labour unions or made progress in gaining education and economic mobility.

Many SC families have left rural areas and come to live in slums and on the pavements in the rapidly growing cities. Here also, they tend to do the worst jobs for the lowest wages. However in some cities, traditional occupations such as being sweepers have been organized in municipal unions and have the advantage of regular work and wages. Most SC workers are casual day labourers, in small factories, quarries and brick kilns or on construction sites, or work as cycle rickshaw drivers or in petty trade. Women and children as well as men work in such jobs but at lower wages. In the large textile mills of Bombay, SC workers have been generally confined to less skilled and less well-paid work. There are, however, growing numbers of SCs in relatively secure areas such as the public services, banking and railways, and sometimes in the private industry. Those resident in the cities have greater access to secondary and higher education and a growing middle class has evolved within the SC community. Discrimination is less evident in the urban areas but residential patterns, particularly in poorer areas, are often on a caste basis.

It needs no emphasis that the efforts made by the state since independence have brought some empowerment of the SCs. However, gaps still exist in almost all social and economic dimensions between the SCs and general population. It should however be pointed out that structural reforms led to encouragement for liberalization, privatization and globalization. Economic liberalism advocates the abolition of government intervention in economic matter. The point to be noted is that in a country where approximately 35 per cent people are illiterate, one cannot avoid state intervention. The above study was an attempt to understand and interpret the present condition of the SCs. In the study it was revealed that still approximately 46 per cent of the SC population is illiterate, while it was only 35 per cent in case of the general population. There is no denying the fact that the dropout rate of SCs for Classes I–V was 32.7 per cent, while it was 31.47 per cent for the general population. In case of secondary education, from I–VIII, it was 55.2 per cent for general and 52.32 per cent for the SCs. For higher secondary, the dropout still increased from I–X it was 69.1 per cent for SCs and for general it was 62.69 per cent. The point to be noted here it that the dropouts show lack of educational development. It may be due the lack of consciousness regarding the importance of education and lower income which has deprived the parents to educate their children.

Further, less than 33 per cent SC households had acquired access to capital assets, compared to 60 per cent among others. About 60 per cent of the SC households have to still depend upon wage labour, compared to the 25 per cent for others. Only 19.99 per cent of the SC population goes for cultivation, while 31.65 per cent of the general population are cultivators. The cause behind this is the massive illiteracy, among SC, law of inheritance, lack of mobility, etc.

The cumulative effect of all these therefore is reflected in high level of poverty. In the year 1993–94, 48.11 per cent of the SC population lived below poverty line; it was 37.50 per cent for other Indians, which declined by 11.31 points in 2004–05 in rural areas for SCs. The decline for other household was 9.00 per cent. That means that even though the poverty ratio was high for SCs living in rural areas, but the decline in poverty was more for SCs. The efforts by the government for reduction of poverty would be appreciated but still lot has to be done because the HDI for SC was 0.303 which is lower than the HDI for non-SC at 0.393 for the period 1980–2000.

The broad Indian reality is that India has too many poor. The value of human poverty ratio was 31.34 per cent for all social groups in India as compared to 41.47 per cent for SCs. Even today, India is predominantly an agrarian economy with over 60 per cent people living in rural areas. No statistics can adequately capture the socio-cultural inequality that is an abiding part of the Indian reality. It has acute inequalities not only in economic terms, but also in the socio-cultural terms.

The free market-oriented reforms ought to take this grave Indian reality into consideration. Unless there is a wide spread of purchasing power in the economy, it can never be sustainable. The reform strategy thus should embody sustainable empowerment of the rural masses; investments to enhance their capability and effective measures for accelerated development of the disadvantaged sections such as Dalits. The prerequisite to reforms therefore could be radical land reforms, massive investments in rural areas into agriculture-related infrastructural projects, primary healthcare system and reinforcement of positive discrimination in favour of Dalits. Still, 80 per cent of the Dalits reside in the rural areas and therefore are not able to take advantage of the positive discrimination which is meant for the upliftment of the Dalits. These facilities are cornered by the people who are well to do. So, it is in the broader national interest that the Government of India should raise the level of investment in the rural areas and provide the facility of vocational training at the primary and secondary levels in order to motivate the parents to educate their children. However, despite the overwhelming odds against them, former "Untouchables" are gaining increasing access to education and their expectations and aspirations are rising. Increasingly, they are refusing to accept their former degraded and subservient position and, if they are able to organize across barriers of language and sub-caste, they will start developing.

It needs no emphasis that the efforts have been made since the First Five-Year Plan for the empowerment of SCs. However, gaps still exist in almost all social and economic dimensions between SCs and the general population. The Eleventh Plan provides an opportunity to restructure policies for faster, more broad-based and inclusive growth. With respect to elementary education, various incentives in the form of abolition of tuition fee, free supply of books, mid-day meals, scholarships and so on shall be provided to the SC children. Among the SCs, children of scavengers are educationally the most backward. The existing Pre-Matric scholarship for them is to be revised in its funding pattern from 50:50 to 100 per cent so that more target families send their children to schools. Special attention needs be paid to retention in schools of SC students and the quality of teaching for them. The scheme of Post-Matric Scholarships for SCs provides scholarships to SC students for pursuing higher education in various courses beyond matriculation. The SC students also need to be encouraged to prepare for various competitive examinations. Reputed institutions charge very high fees for coaching students for competitive examinations. The Rajiv Gandhi National Fellowship for SC students was introduced in 2005–06 to provide fellowship to 1,333 SC students for pursuing higher studies leading to M.Phil. and Ph.D. degrees.

In the Eleventh Plan, a Commission on Land Reforms will be set up which will specifically look into issues of: (i) continued possession and effective uses of land distributed earlier to SCs under various programmes/legislative interventions; and (ii) availability of land for distribution to SCs/STs/landless families. In all these, care will be taken to ensure preferential/joint ownership by women.

The unemployment rate of SCs in rural and urban areas is about 5.5 per cent as against 3.5 per cent for others. Special programmes of employment are necessary to reduce this by increasing employment among SCs. Priority needs to be given to SCs in the Employment Guarantee Scheme with proper monitoring of coverage. The National Sample Survey Organization (NSSO) on Employment and Unemployment Situation among Social Groups in India in its report (61st Round, July 2004–June 2005) brought out that the proportion of persons in the labour force was the highest among STs followed by SCs, OBCs and others. The labour force participation rate for these groups were 51 per cent, 44 per cent and 40 per cent, respectively. Those belonging to the SC communities suffer from very high incidence of poverty and need to be provided with job-oriented training to enable them to have better opportunities.

It should however be pointed out that neo-Buddhists can be a good model for other SCs for their development. During last 60 years, the neo-Buddhists have done a remarkable progress in all walks of life. It was found in the 1971 census that their literacy has become equal to that of the Brahmins and all other castes and SCs lag behind them. The neo-Buddhists have modernized themselves, removed superstitions among themselves and entered into various professions and occupations. They speak on behalf of all the weaker sections. They assert for removal of injustice, equal opportunity, organize them and have a clear perception of development. Now, there are many more doctors, engineers, pleaders, professors, technicians, artists in films and on the stage, administrative officers. They have surpassed the dominant Maratha caste in many respects. They have ably utilized the policy of reservation in particular and policy of protective discrimination in general. They have made use of the Constitution and the political process in an efficient manner. There would be surprise if any other community has made such a remarkable development in such a short period in the history of the world. Progress made by the neo-Buddhists is more because of the strong will for development created by their leader Dr Ambedkar. The spirit among the neo-Buddhists consists of removal of inferiority complex, willingness for hard work, sense of responsibility, etc. This spirit is lacking in other SCs. They may not follow the neo-Buddhists in totality, but the inspiration from them would be very useful for their development. The other SCs should follow this model.

The policy of reservation should be viewed as a part of the total policy for the development. Efforts should be made to observe that it is being implemented sincerely and honestly. However, it would be well to remind us that the reservation would not be enough for the development. Many-sided development, as described above, would be required. An effort should be made to seek help from the liberal Hindus. Contrary to the general belief, there is a strong element of liberalism among the Hindus. Dr Ambedkar made its use wisely in the fight against untouchability. There should be fight against the conservative elements and not all the Hindus. It should not be treated as a cold war between the SCs and the Hindus.

In the post-independence period, every caste is now roughly divided into three classes: the elites, the middle classes and the masses. They have different attitudes. What is necessary are the efforts for the development of the masses in SCs. They badly need it. Globalization has posed a challenge to all and more to the SCs. Unless such efforts are done, the values in the constitution would not be materialized.

Notes

1. Eleventh Five-Year Plan, Vol. I, Planning Commission, Government of India, New Delhi, 2007–12, p. 101.

2. Teltumbde Anand, *Globalisation and Dalits*. Nagpur: Sanket Prakashan, 2001.
3. Elventh Five Year Plan, Planning Commission, Government of India, New Delhi, 2007–08, pp. 106–7.
4. Ibid.
5. Ibid.

References

Dalit and Tribe's blog – Ideology and Ambedkar, www.dalitandtribe.wordpress.com/2010/01/20/ideology-and-ambedkar-by-deepika/

Dubey, Amaresh (2003) Note and Statistical Tables on Social Groups prepared for DIFD, Delhi, quoted by Sukhadeo Thorat "Economic Exclusion and Poverty: Indian Experiences of Remidies Against Exclusion" (conferences.ifpri.org/2020 chinaconferences/pdf/manilac-Thorat.pdf).

Huntington, Samuel P. "The Clash of Civilizations", *Foreign Affairs* 7 (3): 1993 (www.foreignaffairs.com/articles/48950/samuel-phuntington/the-clash-of-civilisation).

Jagan, Karade, ed. *Development of Scheduled Castes and Scheduled Tribes in India*. Cambridge: Scholars Publishing, 2008.

Joshi, V. and M.D. Little. *India's Economic Reforms 1991–2001*. Bombay: Oxford University Press, 1996, 238–39.

National Crime Records Bureau Report (NRCB), Ministry of Home Affairs, 2005.

National Sample Survey Organization on Employment and Unemployment Situation among Social Groups in India in its Report, 61st Round, July 2004–June 2005.

Report of Various Five Year Plans, Planning Commission, Government of India, New Delhi.

8

Youth, Religion and Globalization

Ellina Samantroy

The unprecedented number of young people in the world today can be isolated as one of the crucial reality factors conditioning political and cultural developments. There is no denying the fact that the youth comprise the largest demographic entity in India and are identified as major propellers of social change. The onset of globalization have brought about phenomenal changes in the religious values of the youth. With the youth population burgeoning in India, it has become imperative to explore the concerns, interests and aspirations of youth in the contemporary society. The youth today, are a new kind of population, seeking a universal identity amid pluralities of culture. With growing multi-culturalism, they are ready for change, more adaptable and resilient than the previous generation. There is no denying the fact that they are in a particularly strategic situation who will be most affected by future development and inevitably will be involved in cultural relations. In the contemporary society marked with global flow of ideas and heightened multiculturalism, the modern youth is assailed from every angle by divergent contradictory value claims. Much of the bewilderment of the young and uncertainty stems directly from a decline in religious belief. It is no longer possible, as it was in the not too distant historical past, to setting comfortably into the value system of one's forbearers or one's community and live without one's life without ever examining the nature and the assumption of the system. One natural result of this uncertainty and confusion is that there is an increasing concern about, interest in, and a searching for, sound or meaningful value approach which can hold its own in today's world. As a consequence of westernization and globalization our country is undergoing bewildering metamorphosis. The traditional ties and value system are undergoing changes and the youth are most affected, so the traditional ties value also change drastically. Religion, one of our major institutions which are seen as formal structural operating to solve persistent social problems has tremendously lost its significance. The word "religion" implies the consciousness of our manifold and constitutive bonds; our links with body, soul and spirit; our link with the entire humanity; our link to the entire earth and the whole creation; and our link with that mystery one of whose symbols is the Divine. So, a religious person is someone who is conscious of all his connections with the entire universe, aware of all the links which relate a person to the whole reality, a fellow being of our universe.

In a society such as ours which is under the onslaught of heightened consumerism driven by technology, the rapid rate of change is unprecedented and relatively unchecked by morality. Inevitably, it seems any change affects the young more than the old. In fact, the young arguably constitute that portion of the population most affected by globalization, both because the economic practises of late capitalism target adolescent to socialize them into the value of consumerism and because globalization presents serious challenges to identify, the development of which is necessary for every youth.

Globalization and Religion

In a globalized world, the search for identity is also global and the religious currents form an alternative perspective trying to locate their identity in a changing world. Under the global circumstances, both dominant suppositions and alternative suppositions which challenge them influence "the trajectories of globalisation" (Robertson, 1992: 68). Robertson insists that identity is pursued in terms of ideas about tradition, history, locality, community and nation which have been globally diffused. Today, religious currents must be understood as expressions of their place within the global field. The social and cultural theorists have focussed on such implications of globalization. As Peter Beyer writes, "the power of ... technology makes very rapid communication possible over almost unlimited space. Moreover, (the new) media exist nearly everywhere on earth, along with the will and ability to use them. The potential for worldwide communication has been translated into actual practice. We therefore live in a globalising social reality, one in which previously effective barriers to communication no longer exist" (1994: 1). Further Beyer argues, "people, cultures, societies and civilisations previously more or less isolated from one another are now in regular, almost unavoidable, contact" (ibid.).

In this context, national borders become less significant and the forces of globalization transcend all boundaries. Moreover, these changes have a profound influence on religion as there is contraction of social space and greater awareness of the diversity of human experience, challenging many local belief systems and worldviews. For Beyer, globality implies completion of "mission". Under the new circumstances, "the crystallisation of telic concerns" that characterizes globalization provides an appropriate medium for world theologies that address "the eschatological implications of an inclusive humanity" (ibid.: 30). The universalism of religion, it is argued, meets the global at the level of world inclusiveness. The modern order has brought intense pressure to bear upon the older worldviews; at the same time it has offered them vast new potentials. A globalized world, in short, supercharges religion. Finally, Beyer argues, religion has become a "proactive force". It is now "instrumental" in the elaboration and development of globalization (ibid.).

Globalization, Youth Culture and Religious Beliefs

Sociologists have increasingly concerned themselves with the study of "youth culture" since many years. One of the influential articles of Talcott Parsons characterizing youth culture as "more or less specifically irresponsible" (1942) has become a point of departure for an enormous amount of research and discussion on youth. Youth culture, as Eisenstadt (2003) shows, is a mode of accommodation to the stresses caused by discontinuity between early learning and expectations, and later experiences. But, the culture of modern youth itself is important not only for its functions and form, but for its content. Myers says, "first whatever is coming probably will contain an alternative to the free market as we know it today ... secondly, globalism does not provide a satisfactory home for the individual being. The market may be global, the technology may be global but I never will be. Human beings need a place, a story, a set of relationships. This is why ethnicity and religion are emerging as such powerful counter forces to globalism today" (Myers, 1998).

However, it can be said that young India faces the global world with more handicaps than its major Asian competitors such as China. On the one hand, in India, the modern youth are witnessing a rapid change in lifestyle, ideology, culture and value preferences; on the other hand, this new generation is quite conservative when it comes to changing certain value preferences and ideology with regard to religion. Being religious has become a new kind of dissent, a moral testament, and it so effortlessly co-exists with reason and doubt, knowledge and technology. The religious practice in India presently does not correspond to the western notions of "conservative" or "liberal". Religious observance clearly remains an important part in the lives of the young people throughout the country, as reflected in visits to places of worship and observance of fasts. What we call progress in science and economics has not exiled God from the mind or the market place. The new revolutions, staged in the windowless chambers of information technology, like the old ones, promise heaven on earth – or the last kingdom of happiness. Then why is God not redundant? In fact, it is a celebration of harmony between, man, machine and the mystery of being. Progress in "material culture" as Ogburn would consider, being very rapid does not in fact, destroy the "non-material culture". A larger truth, typically an Indian one, lies here, i.e., in the age of state-sponsored theology of secularism; it is not a Herculean task to be religious. In fact, as Professor Dipankar Gupta would argue, "it is necessary to distinguish between belief in god and in religious rituals ... to faithfully observe rituals one has to be religious, but not all religious people need to be ritualistic". Today, what we consider as being religious is observing fasts or visiting places of worship is simply a ritual practice rather than belief in the almighty or understanding the true ethos of religion. What is even more surprising is that today's youth think in as staid, a fashion. Religious symbols are becoming cultural accessories.

Globalization, Religion and Cultural Identities of the Youth

Today, people are choosing, much like everything else in their lives, their religious identities. Madonna and some other pop stars would wear a cross as a fashion accessory rather than to show a devout state of mind. Secular radicalism is in combat with the essential cultural characteristics of India, and redeemingly, the young Indian is not such a radical. India is a religious society, and like its dominant religion, it is neither linear nor dogmatic. It is this freedom never available in an ideology that makes being religious and being young compatible. Today, there is a great desire for freedom in youth and a desire for the experience of community. But such a desire is quite contrary to the Durkheimian notion of "collective conscience" reinforced by religion. The freedom soughlt is freedom from the authority of adults, and the community sought is usually a community of coveals. In fact, most of these desires of the modern youth find the traditions of the adult society uncongenial. The remarkable thing to be understood is how much, despite its reluctance, youth assimilates of those traditions.

Mannheim (1997) claimed that generations, radicalized by traumatic experiences, could transform the society by challenging customary thought and offering new political and cultural visitors. The views of religion are less relevant to the modern societies which have multiple sub-cultures and varied realities. It is a characteristic of the modern societies that the strength of the traditions centring about authority have been resented, and powerful tendencies to overcome them have become prominent and even relatively successful. It is a belief that much of what has been accepted as valid belief in the past, and even at present, might be wrong and is susceptible of being improved by more valid knowledge; it is a belief that modes of action and techniques of control of nature have often been wrong and inadequate and should be displaced by better ones which are more congenial to desire and more effective in the attainment of accepted ends, such as material well-being and the freedom of the individual to act in accordance to spontaneous desire and desire regulated by reason.

The globalization of economy and the decentralization of production of goods and services by the multinational corporations has totally altered for these youth the project of their future and the perception of their "life-world". With the modern youth existing in "multiple realities" and experiencing a plurality of "life-worlds", it becomes difficult to understand the significance of religious values on them. They fail to realize and understand the value of religious instruction as an agency of socialization. Even Arnold W. Green's mention of the universal functions of religion "as that which rationalises and makes bearable individual suffering in the known world ... as that which helps to knit the social values of a society into a cohesive whole" is not properly internalized by the modern youth (Green, 1956).

Therefore, the global cosmopolitan environment may socialize the adolescents into the norms of the global community but it is the responsibility of the adolescent to resist those norms until they can be freely choosen after mastering subsequent skills to understand the dilemmas of global culture.

Conclusion

The above discussion reflects on the flexibility of religious belief and practices in a globalized era. To be very precise, religion can be a matter of personal experience. While in some circumstances, religion may appear to operate as a mechanism of social control and integration, while in the other, it may appear to sanction both domination and liberation within the same context. Therefore, in order to comprehend the true character of religion, it is important to place it in the appropriate socio-economic, political and cultural contexts. To quote Robertson in his analysis of cultural phenomena that "uniqueness simply cannot be regarded as a thing in itself. It largely depends on both the thematisation and diffusion of 'universal' ideas concerning the appropriateness of being unique in a context, which is an empirical matter, and the employment of criteria on the part of scholarly observers, which is an analytical issue" (Robertson, 1992: 130). So, in order to understand the uniqueness of religion, it should be expressed within the trajectories of both local and global. Since global accounts in general evacuate beliefs, practices and institutions of their specific significance, leaving religion as little more than a reference to the whole or to traditions of the supernatural, sacred, super-empirical or transcendent.

The youth seem to be taking refuge in the traditional, using cultural and religious security blankets to protect themselves from the sudden, strident onslaught of a lifestyle and choices that they have not been used to or that are alien to Indian culture. But instead of using religion as a staid or fashion, the youth should strive for this global culture and resist the burden of excessive consumerism and technologization. They should consider religion as a "proactive force". The future torch bearers of our country need to live and experience this global culture and locate religion amid diversity of life-worlds, thereby not altering their identity. They need to explore and understand to cope up with the resistance the post-modern world imposes on them.

References

Beyer, P. *Religion and Globalization*. London: Sage, 1994.

Eisenstadt, S.N. *From Generation to Generation*, New Brunswick, New Jersey: Transaction Publishers, 2003.

Green, A.W. *Sociology*. New York: McGraw Hill, 1956.

Gupta, D. "The Old-fashioned Young", *India Today*, XXX (4): 89, 25–31 January 2005.

Mannheim, K. "The Problem of Generations", in *Collected Works of Karl Mannheim*, London: Routledge, 1997.

Myers, B. "What is Going On?", *MARC Newsletter* 98 (4), 1998: 3–4.

Pannikar, R. "Recovering Religion", *Times of India*, 28 January 2006.

Parsons, T. "Age and Sex in the Social Structure of the United States", *American Sociological Review*, October 1942.

Robertson, R. *Globalization: Social Theory and Global Culture*. London: Sage, 1992.

Index